BLUEPRINTS

Health Education Key Stage 2 Copymasters

John Lloyd

Ron Morton

Stanley Thornes (Publishers) Ltd

Illustrations by Kim Blundell

First published in 1992 by:
Stanley Thornes (Publishers) Ltd
Ellenborough House
Wellington Street
CHELTENHAM GL50 1YD

Reprinted 1993

A catalogue record for this book is available from the British Library.

ISBN 0–7487–1476–6

Typeset by Tech-Set, Gateshead, Tyne & Wear
Printed in Great Britain at The Bath Press, Avon

CONTENTS

The health promoting school

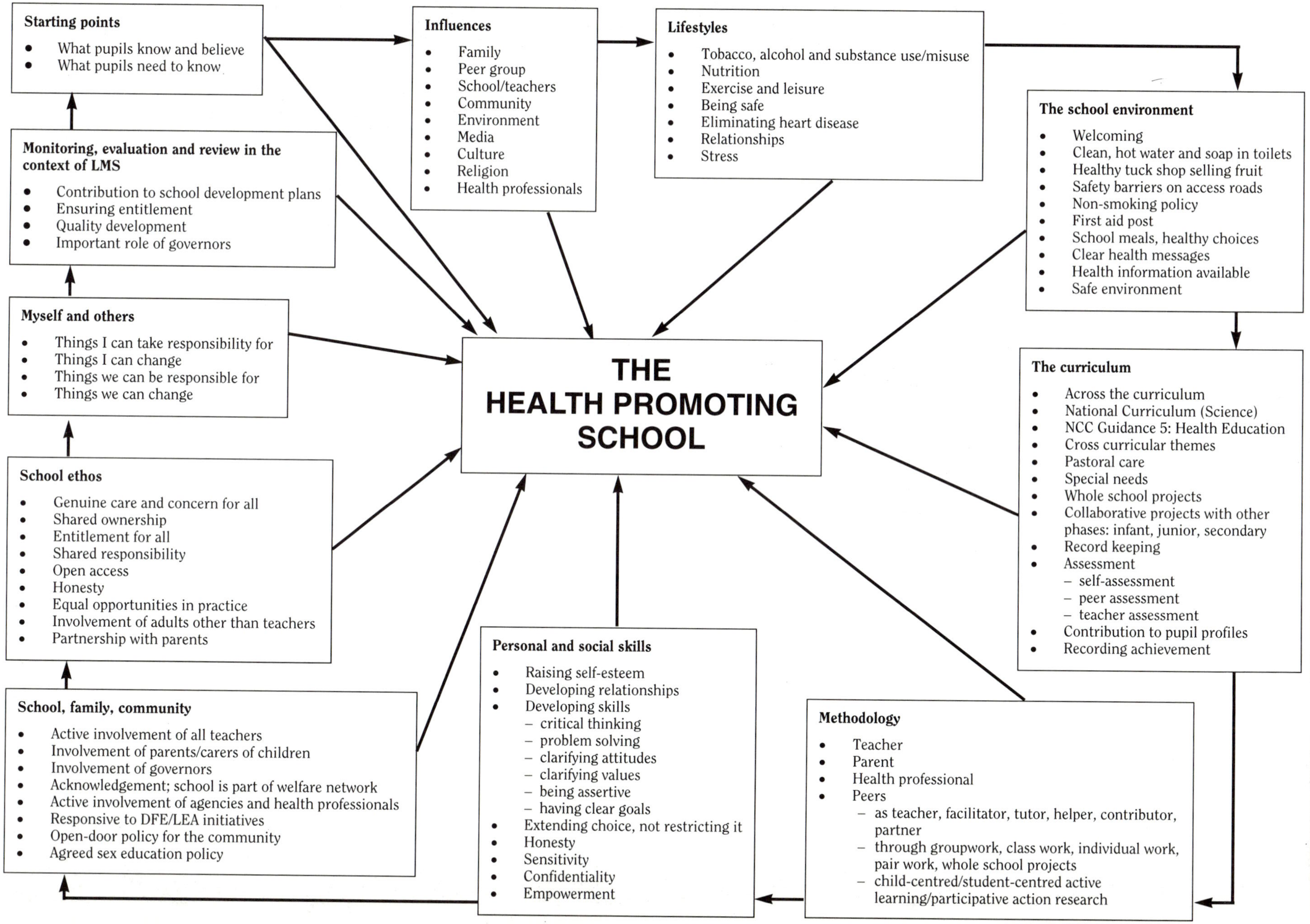

Natural remedies

Name of plant	Name of substance	Used in the treatment of
e.g. Poppy	Opium	anaesthetic/ painkiller
1		
2		
3		
4		
5		

How many can you find?

Digitalis purpurea

Medicine chest

cough medicine

antiseptic cream

inhaler

aspirin

foot powder

Milk of Magnesia

Alexander Fleming

Alexander Fleming discovered the drug penicillin quite by accident. He was growing a colony of bacteria in his laboratory in 1928 when he noticed on one particular growth culture that some mould had grown. When he examined it closely he realised that the bacteria around the mould were dead. Fleming grew some more of this mould called **penicillin notatum** and tried it out on different types of bacteria which caused disease. He found that it killed these bacteria also.

Penicillin became a 'wonder drug' during the Second World War when it was manufactured in large quantities to treat soldiers wounded in battle. Penicillin saved thousands of lives because it prevented the spread of infections from wounds. Since the war many penicillin type drugs have been developed.

Now answer these questions in your workbook.

- Why was the discovery of penicillin an accident?
- Why was penicillin called a 'wonder drug'?
- When was penicillin first manufactured in quantity and why?
- How did Alexander Fleming check that the mould actually killed bacteria that caused disease?
- Imagine that you are Alexander Fleming. Write a short paragraph to explain what you were doing, what you saw and what conclusions you made.

The long way home

C4

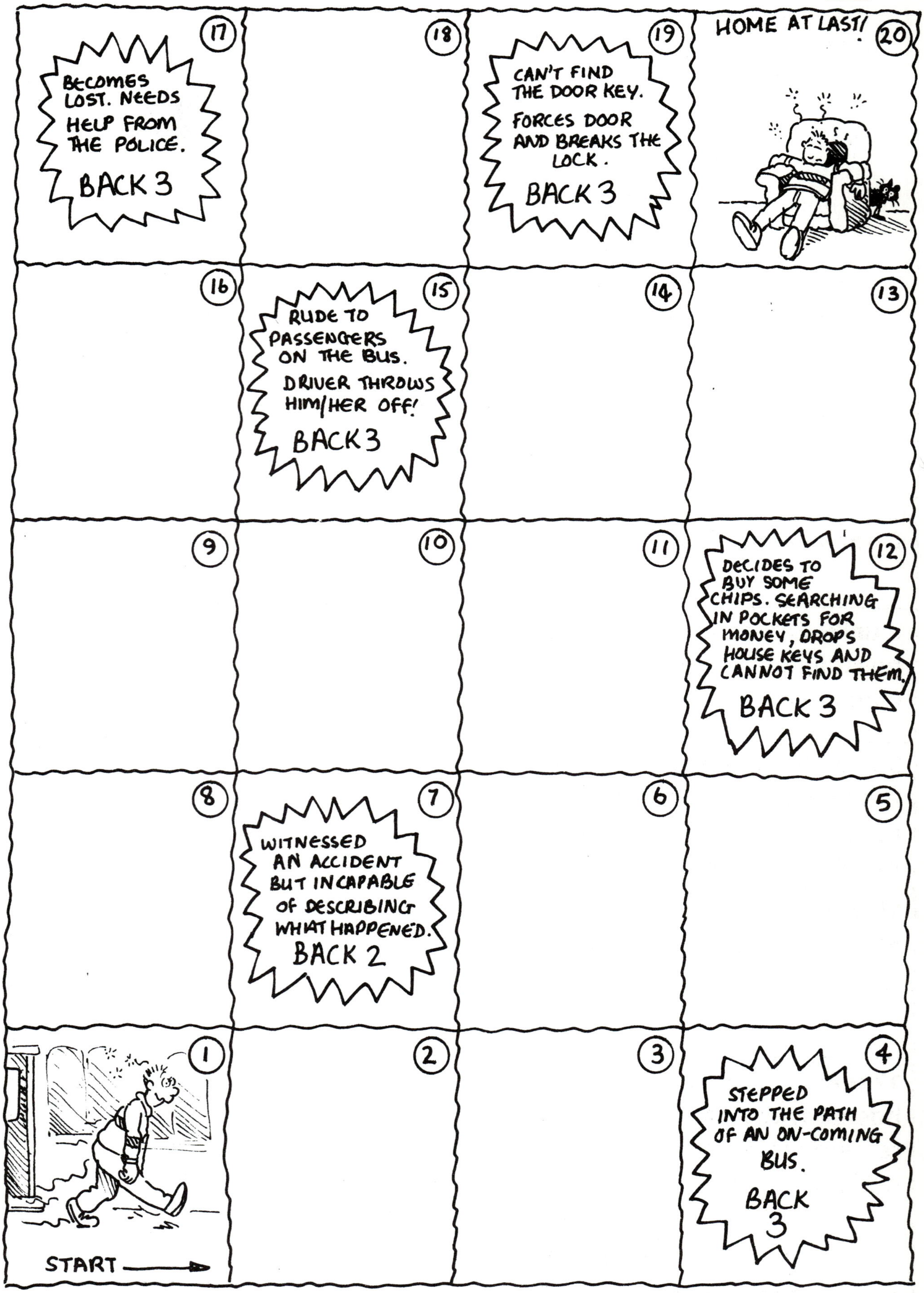

Units of alcohol

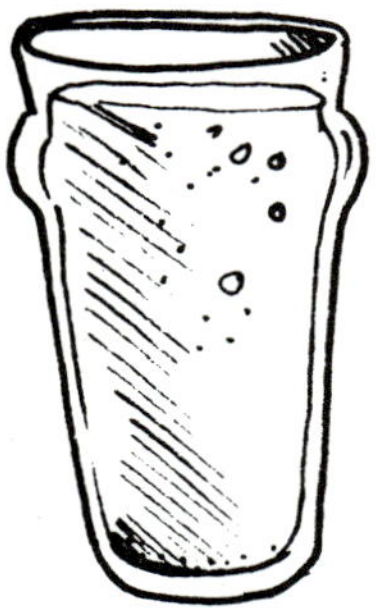

Half a pint of beer

or

1 single spirit (whisky, vodka, gin, brandy)

or

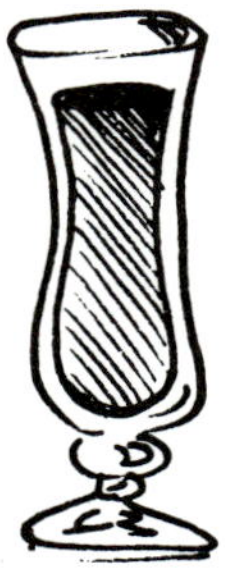

1 glass of sherry or port

or

1 glass of wine

= **1 unit of alcohol**

(the amount that can be processed by the liver in an hour)

2 units Person feels relaxed.	
3 units Person begins to be talkative, possibly loud and excited. Greater chance of accidents occurring.	
5 units Person has difficulty in moving normally and in a controlled way. Reactions to events are slower.	
10 units Person is likely to be drunk and will be unable to walk properly.	
12 units Person suffers double vision, has difficulty speaking and remembering, could become angry and be very sick.	

Fermentation

Labels

C7

Name of medicine	Measure (units) ml/mg/gm	Dose per day	Quantity (total)	Form (tablets, cream, liquid	Date	Name of patient

The world

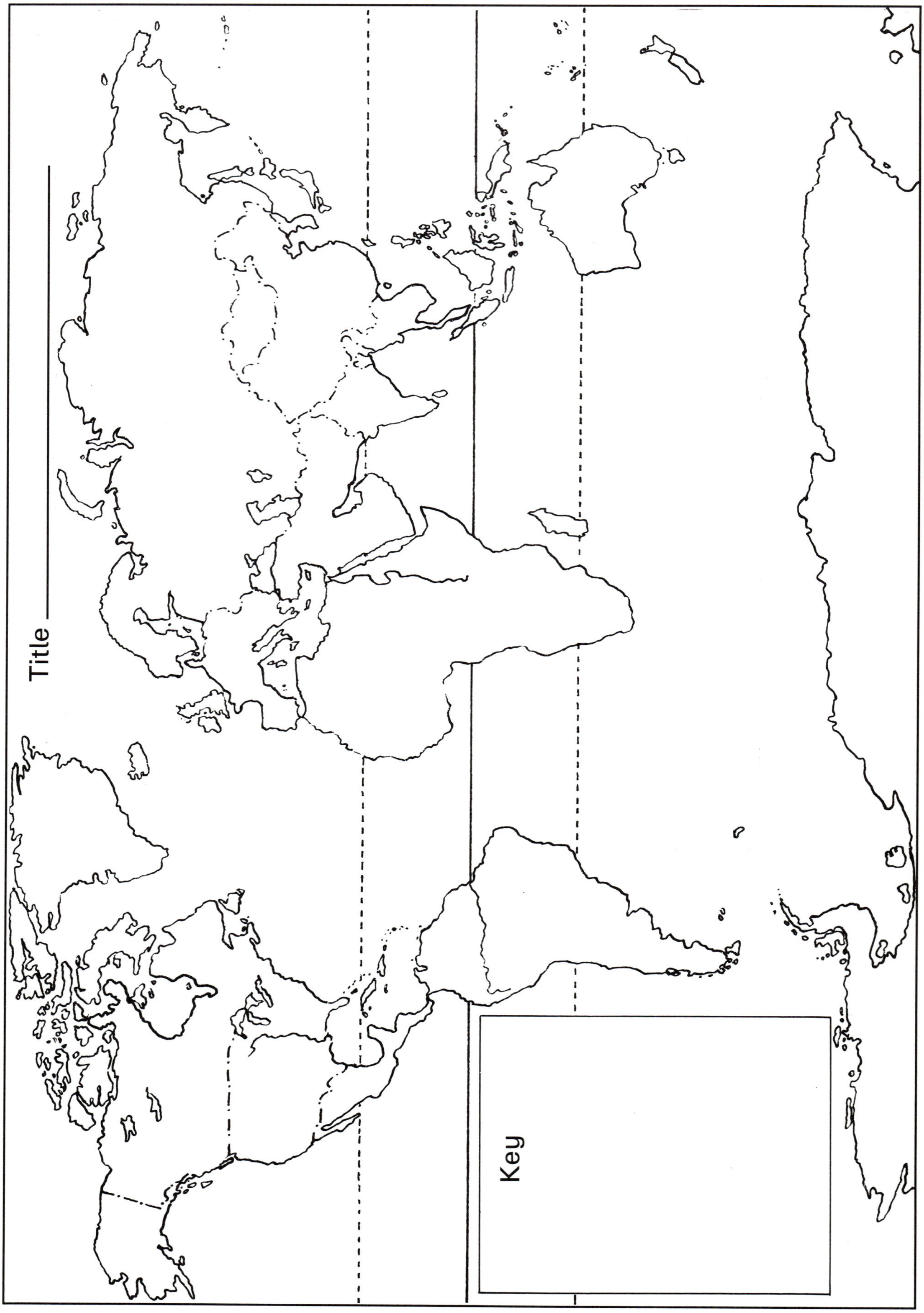

Map of South America

Drug run

Enough coca leaves are grown in Peru to make 1 kg of cocaine worth £500.

1 kg of smuggled cocaine is worth £2,500.

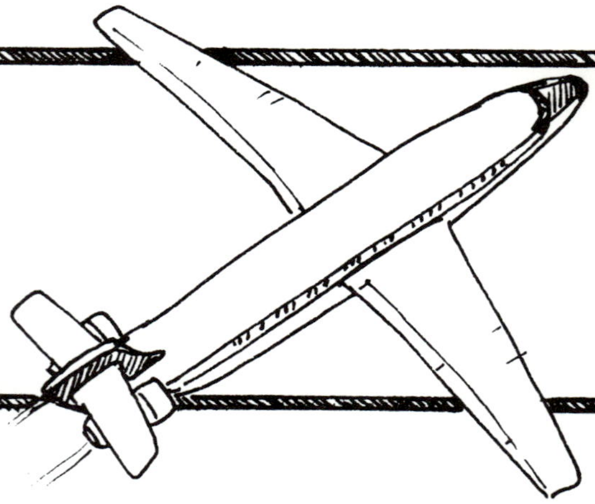

Dealers sell 1 kg of cocaine for £30,000. Sometimes cocaine is turned into another drug called crack which can be smoked.

A drug user pays between £80 and £100 for a gram of cocaine. The street value of 1 kg is over £80,000. Cocaine is usually 'sniffed' by drug users. This stimulates them and makes them feel good. However, they need more and more cocaine to get the same thrill repeatedly. Continued heavy use can cause depression and feelings of anxiety and even panic.

Is it really worth it?

Needle sharp technology

C12

In order to show how you would make a model of a syringe, you have to consider things very carefully. Through words and/or drawings, show what needs to be done to make a model syringe.

1) Write/draw whatever you know about injections and syringes: who uses them, why and how.

2) Write/draw an explanation stating how your model will work.

3) Show what a plan to make your syringe will look like. List the materials you need to make your model.

4) Does your model work? Make a list of questions you need to ask that will test whether your model works.

Comic strip

Something I learned

C14

Something I learned about alcohol is ______________________________

____

____.

Something I learned about medicines from the past is ____________

____

____.

Something I learned about illegal drugs is ______________________

____

____.

____

____

____.

Something positive/good about drugs is ________________________

____

____.

Something I learned about saying 'no' is ______________________

____

____.

Something I enjoyed about **Medicines and drugs** is ____________

____

____.

Changes

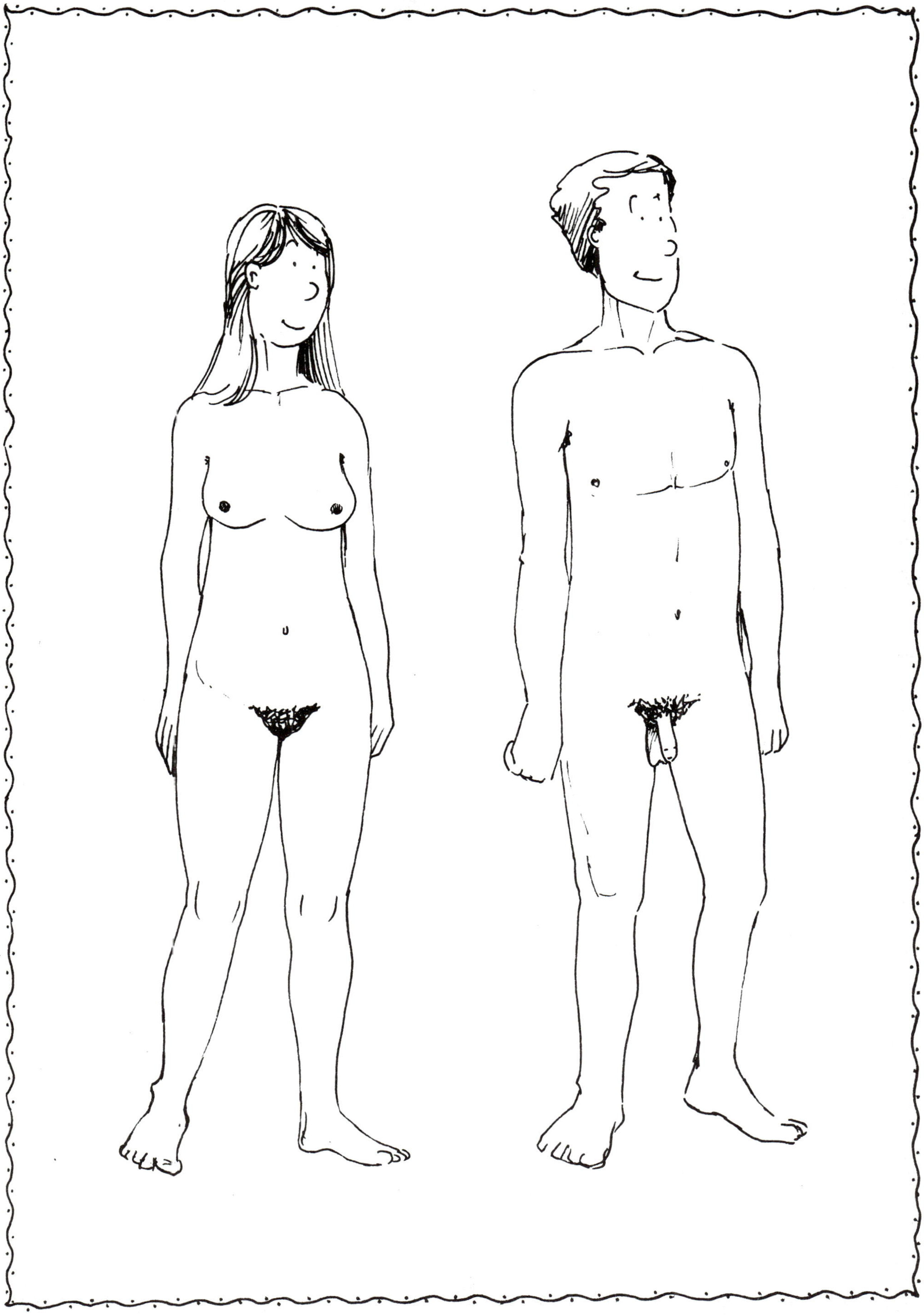

Female reproductive organs

Using the words listed, label the diagrams correctly. In the space available briefly describe what happens to girls during puberty.

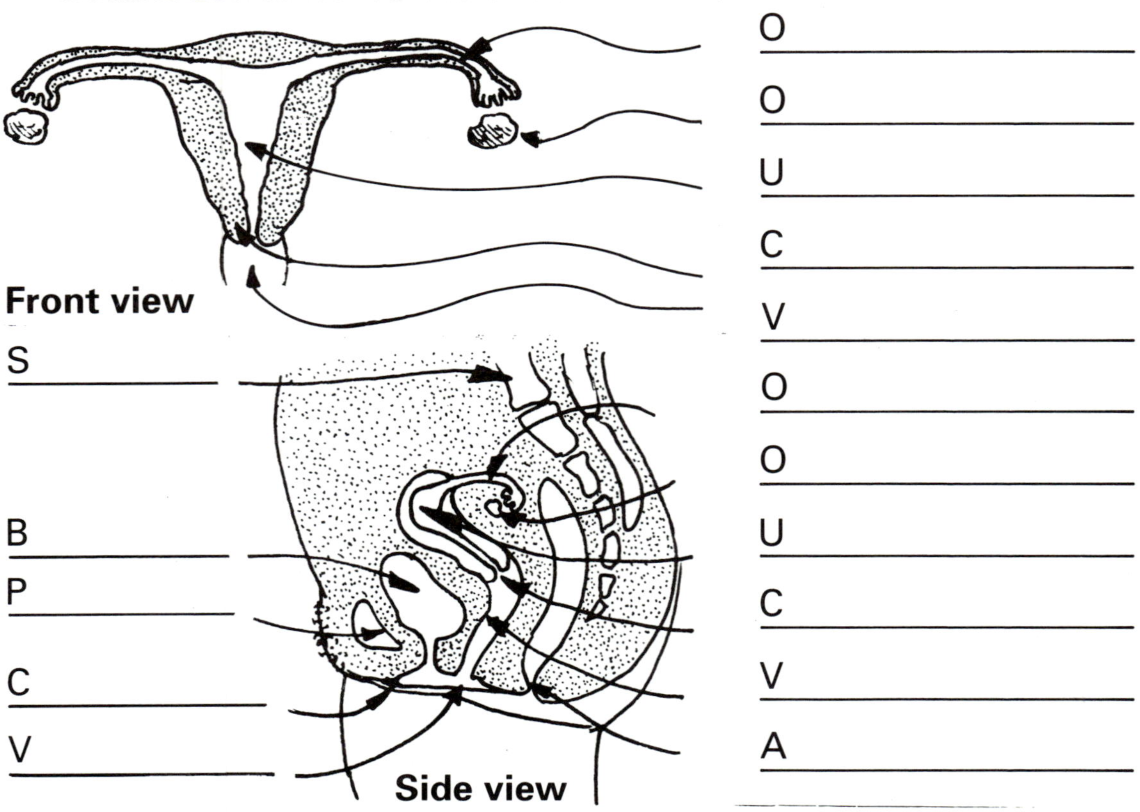

WORDS

pubic bone ovary vagina bladder clitoris

spine uterus vulva oviduct cervix

PUBERTY

Male reproductive organs

Using the words listed, label the diagram correctly. In the space available briefly describe what happens to boys during puberty.

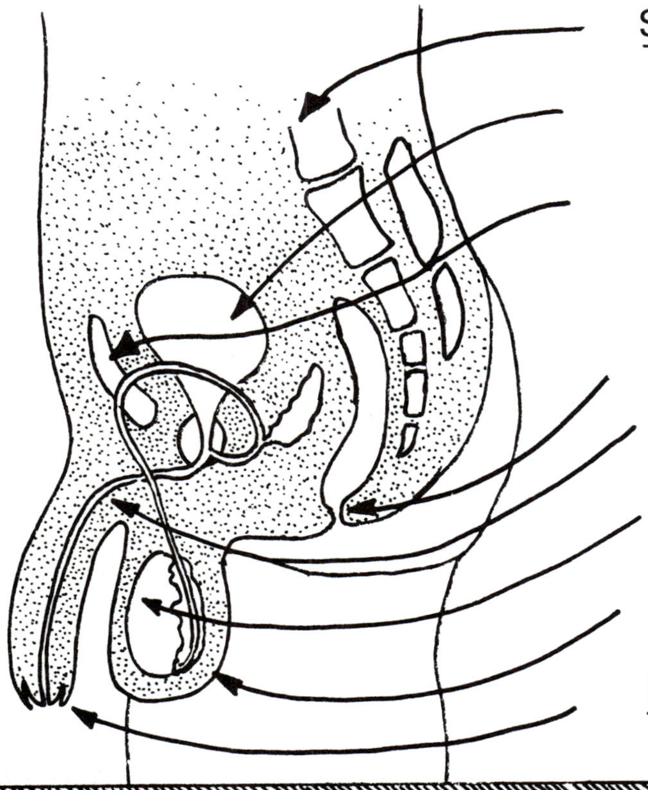

S ______________________

B ______________________

P ______________________

A ______________________

U ______________________

T ______________________

S ______________________

P ______________________

WORDS

testicle scrotum spine urethra bladder penis pubic bone anus

PUBERTY

Human reproduction

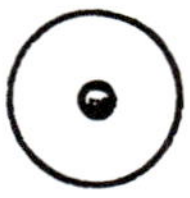

ova (egg)

- female
- 0.1 mm
- 1 only

sperm

- male
- microscopic
- millions

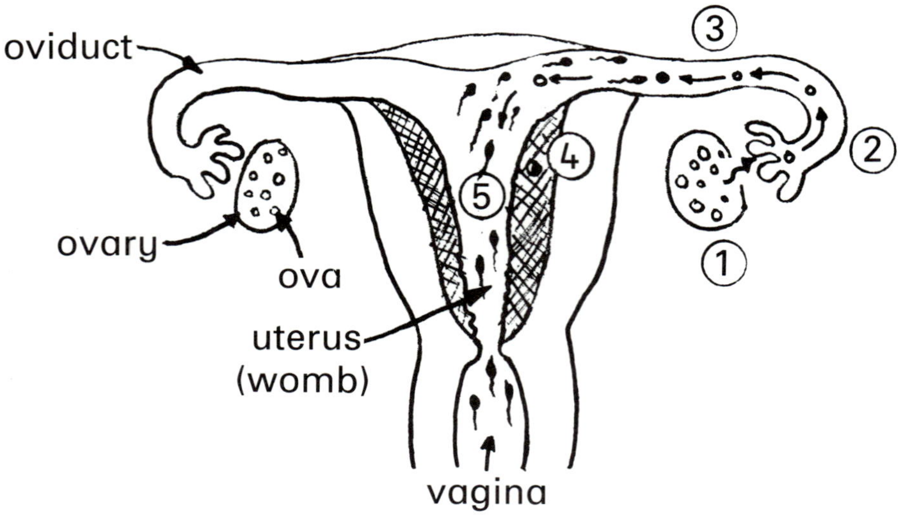

1) An egg is released from the ovary.
2) The egg enters the oviduct.
3) The egg is fertilised by a single sperm swimming up from the vagina.
4) The fertilised egg embeds itself in the rich lining of the womb.
5) Millions of sperm 'swim' into the uterus from the vagina after sexual intercourse.

- It will take nine months for the baby to grow and develop before it is ready to be born.
- It is very important that babies are born into families where they can be cared for physically and emotionally. Parents, Mum and Dad, need to spend a great deal of time with babies, loving and caring for them. This care is essential if babies are to grow into healthy children. Having babies costs a lot of money too!

Equal opportunities charter

Mega cities

Mega city	Country	Continent	Population
○ Sao Paulo			
○ New York			
○ Shanghai			
○ Cairo			
○ Paris			
○ London			
○ Mexico City			
○			
○			
○			

Use your atlas to locate these cities. Can you find out how many people live there? Can you identify any other mega cities?

Stages of growth

After _____ weeks of pregnancy the foetus is recognisably human and is about _____ mm long. Its toes and fingers are still webbed and its head is large compared to the rest of its body.

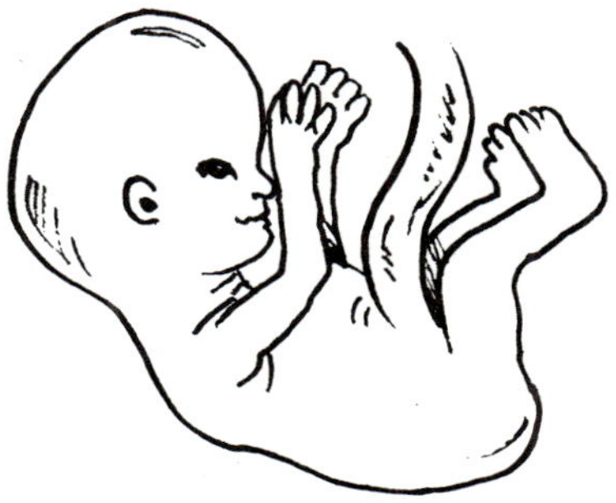

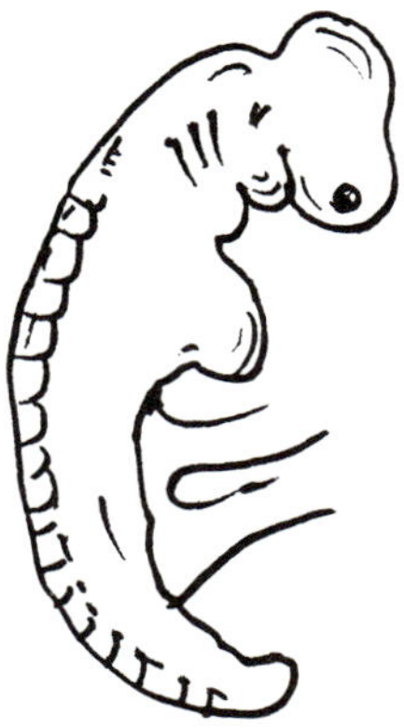

_____ weeks after sperm has fertilised the ovum in the womb, the embryo is _____ mm long, has a head, tail and a basic brain as well as a beating heart. Tiny buds are beginning to appear; these are the start of limbs.

Following _____ weeks after conception the embryo is _____ mm long and has basic internal organs, the eyes and ears are visibly forming and limb joints and facial features are recognisable.

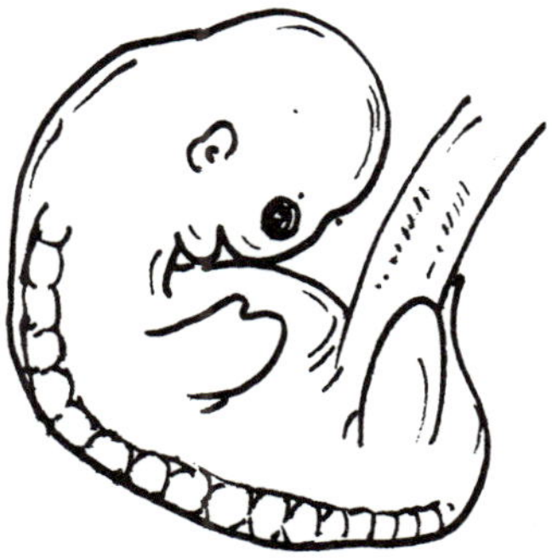

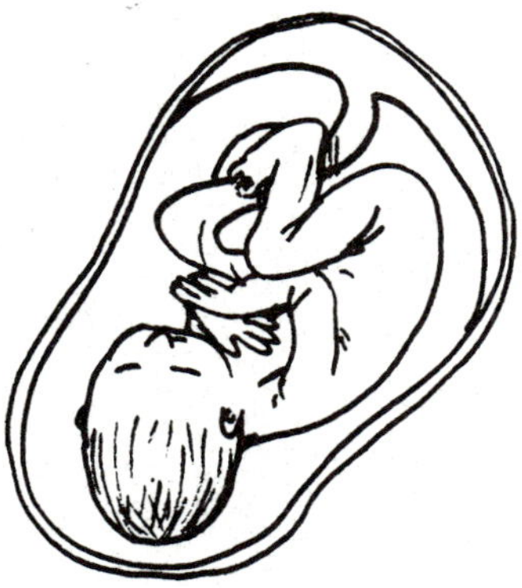

By _____ week the movements of the foetus are very noticeable and can be felt through the wall of the mother's tummy.

Rate of growth

Rate of growth in the early stages of human development

1) Mark the following co-ordinates on the graph below:

   6 mm (4 weeks)

   22 mm (6 weeks)

   50 mm (13 weeks)

   100 mm (16 weeks).

2) Draw a line graph to show the rate of growth.

3) Mark the anticipated length of the baby after 8, 10, 11 and 14 weeks following conception.

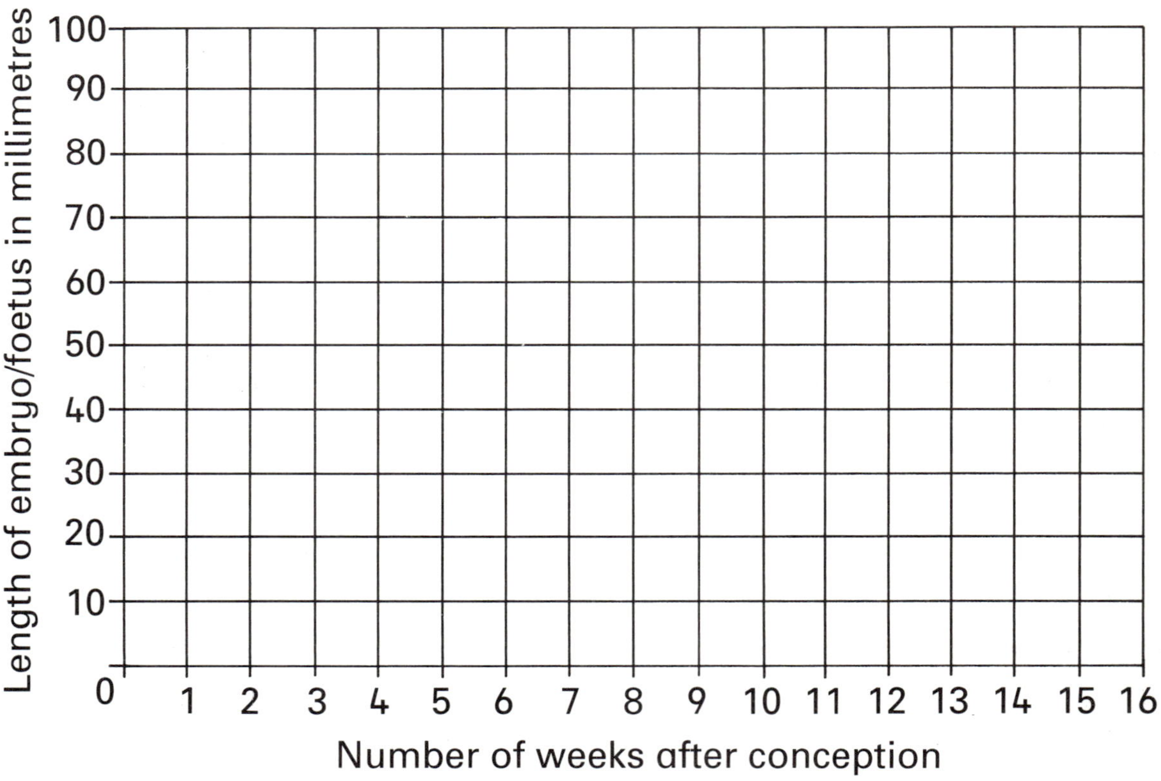

Rites of passage

Religion	Birth	Initiation into faith	Marriage	Death
Sikh				
Christian				
Jewish				
Muslim				
Other				

Making vows

Making decisions

When I am older I might decide to

Something about me

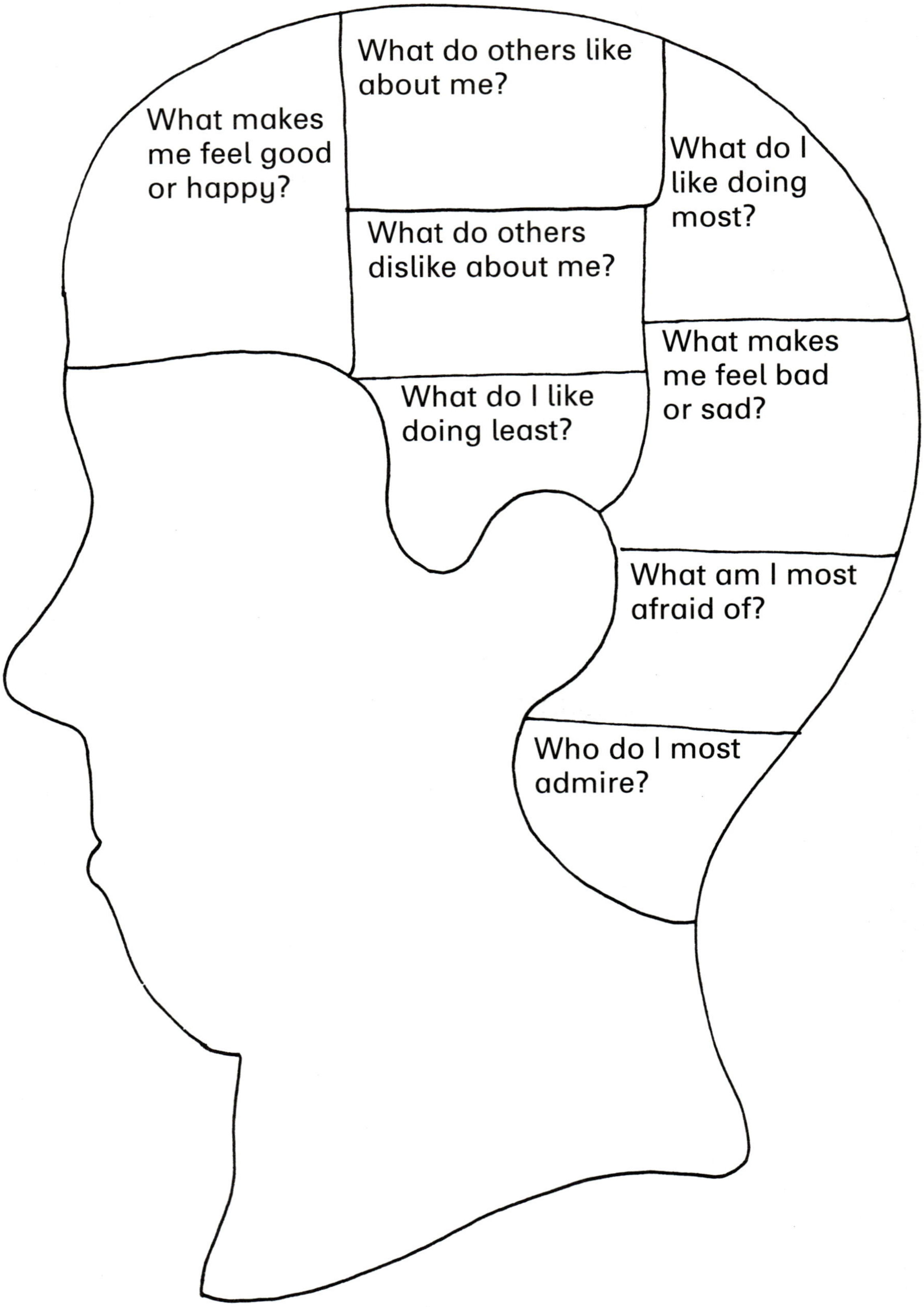

Problem page

Consider the problems described below. What would you advise? Write your answers in the spaces provided.

Dear Jason and Julie,
My best friend has suddenly dumped me and is now not speaking to me. I can't think why she has done this. Now I can't stand going to school and don't know who to turn to. There is a boy in our class who seems quite friendly with both of us but I don't want to talk to him about it in case he stops speaking to me. What can I do?
Yours sincerely
Dawn

Dear Dawn

Yours
Jason and Julie

Dear Jason and Julie
After P.E last week some boys started to laugh at me. They said I was skinny and the size of a titch. They said that I looked ugly because my ears stick out and my teeth are wonky. Now all they do is call me names and push me about. Have you any ideas about what I should do? I can't take much more of this.
Yours hopefully
Omar.

Dear Omar

Yours
Jason and Julie

Dear Jason and Julie
My mum and Dad say I'm too young to come home from the Youth Club on my own even though it finishes at 9.30. I'm twelve years old and know the way home blindfolded. Also I feel really daft going to meet my Dad sitting in his clapped out Metro. It's a real embarrassment. What can I do to persuade them to let me come home on my own?
Yours sincerely
Jilly.

Dear Jilly

Yours
Jason and Julie

My family diary (1)

Monday

An important thing for my family today was ______________________________

______________________________.

What I liked most today was ______

____

______________________________.

What I liked least today was ______

____

______________________________.

Today I felt ______________________

______________________________.

Something I would change is ______

____

______________________________.

Tuesday

Wednesday

Thursday

My family diary (2)

Friday

Saturday

Sunday

Summary

The best day of the week was

____________________ because

____

____________________________.

The day I liked least was

____________________ because

____

____________________________.

The day I would change is

____________________ because

____

____________________________.

Choosing a gift

Choose a gift for a child of a given age. Draw the gifts in the boxes below.

6 months	12 months	24 months
36 months	48 months	60 months

Family problems (1): questions

? **Maths** Grandpa is coming to live with the family. James has a room which measures 3.5 m × 3 m and his sister Katie has a room measuring 4 m × 4.5 m. How much bigger is Katie's room than James's?

Health Why does their mother think a larger room will be better for Grandpa?

? **Maths** Before baby Jake was born the Williams family received Family Allowance worth £8.00 for James, the eldest, and £7.00 for Katie. When Jake was born the family received the same as for Katie. How much Family Allowance do they receive each week?

Health Why do families receive Family Allowance for children? How might children's health benefit from it?

? **Maths** Mrs Williams was discussing with her sister Doreen how James who is nine is 120 cm tall, whereas his cousin George, who is the same age, is only three quarters that height. How tall is George?

Health Has James's Aunt Doreen any reason to worry about George's height?

? **Maths** Aunt Doreen smokes 15 cigarettes a day. Over a month (31 days) Dad reckoned that at £1.50 for a packet of 20, Aunt Doreen's habit is costing her a fortune. How much does Aunt Doreen spend each month on cigarettes?

Health It is not just the cost of Aunt Doreen's smoking that worries the family; what else is it? What can they do about her smoking habit?

Family problems (1): answers

✓ **Maths**	**Health**
✓ **Maths**	**Health**
✓ **Maths**	**Health**
✓ **Maths**	**Health**

Family problems (2): questions

? **Maths** Dad came home from the doctor where he was told he was overweight. For his height he should weigh 78 kilos but he weighs 92 kilos. How much overweight is he?

Health What can his family do to help him lose weight?

? **Maths** The weekly household bill for the Williams family is as follows:

food	£60.00	electricity	£12.45
gas	£10.50	fares/petrol	£20.30
clothes	£12.60	papers/comics	£3.35
school dinners	£9.60	other	£5.80

What is the total?

Health Mr and Mrs Williams need to save at least £30.00 per week and have to cut back from their spending. Where can they make savings that will not affect the health and well-being of the family?

? **Maths** The Williams family – three children, Mum, Dad and Grandpa – want to go on holiday. The holiday will cost £900.00. Jake, the baby, goes free. James counts as an adult although Katie goes at half price. How much is the cost of an adult fare?

Health Why might taking a holiday be good for a family?

? **Maths** Grandpa has to take 3 tablets at 3 hourly intervals, 4 times a day. How many tablets will he take each day? If he starts at 9.30a.m., at what times during the day will he take his tablets?

Health What can a family do to ensure that medicines in the home are kept safe?

Family problems (2): answers

✓ Maths	Health
✓ Maths	Health
✓ Maths	Health
✓ Maths	Health

Working families

Poor housing means a family's health ______________________________ .

Good housing means a family's health ______________________________ .

A decent wage means a family's health ______________________________ .

Poor wages means a family's health ______________________________ .

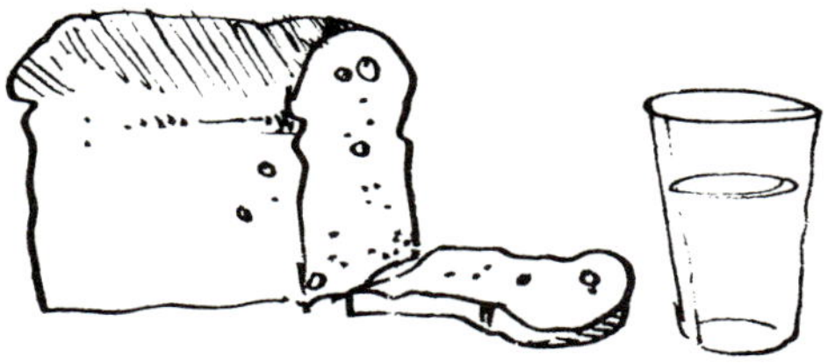

Little food means a family's health ______________________________ .

Nourishing food means a family's health ______________________________ .

A helping hand

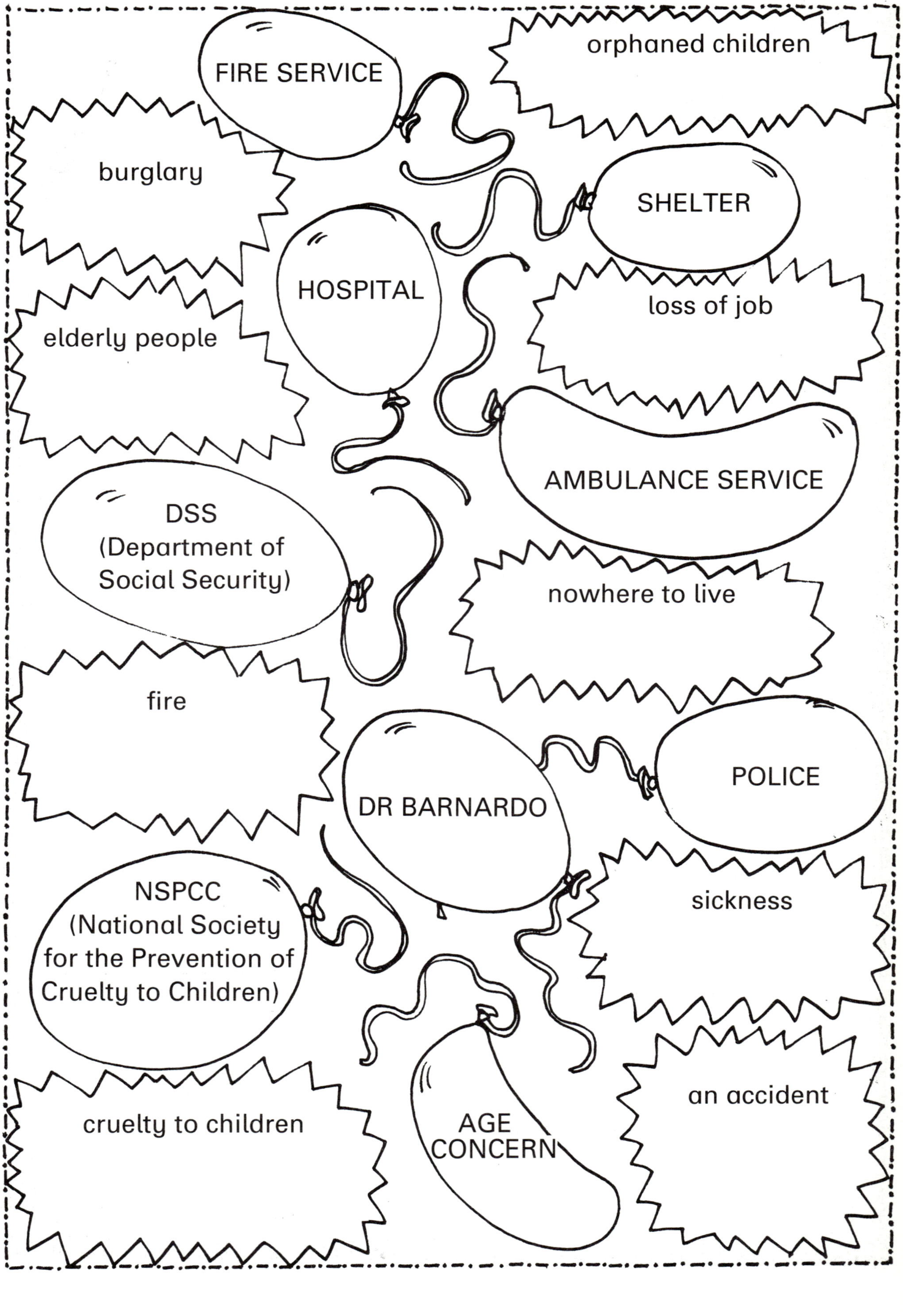

Valuing the elderly

A CHARTER FOR THE ELDERLY

All elderly people are entitled to

____

____.

All elderly people are entitled to

____

____.

All elderly people are entitled to

____

____.

All elderly people are entitled to

____

____.

All elderly people are entitled to

____

____.

Signed ______________________

My family song

My commemorative plaque

My family achievements

I am called ______________________________. I am in class ________.

Things I can do for myself are ____________________________________

____.

Things I do for my family are

____

____

______________________________.

Things I do with my family are

____

____

______________________________.

Something I am proud of is ____

____.

What I like most about my family is ______________________

____

______________________________.

I would like to ______________________

____

____

______________________________.

I wish I could ____

____.

I am going to ____

____.

Threats

Dangers

People	Home	Road	Railways	Play areas	Water	Medicines and drugs	Bullies	Strangers	People we know	School
1										
2										
3										
4										
5										
6										
7										
8										
9										
10										
11										
12										
13										
14										
15										
16										
17										
18										
19										
20										

Disasters

1883 Victoria Hall, Sunderland: 183 die due to panic. ☐

1347–50 British Isles, Black Death: 800,000 die due to plague. ☐

1945 Hiroshima, Japan: 141,000 die due to atomic explosion. ☐

1846–51 Ireland: 1,500,000 die due to famine. ☐

TIME —————————— LINE

1665 London: 68,000 die due to plague carried by rats. ☐

1969–71 North China (reported 1981): 20,000,000 die due to famine. ☐

AD79 Pompeii: entire town buried by volcanic eruption. ☐

1982 Salarg Tunnel, Afghanistan: 1,100 die due to petrol tanker explosion. ☐

Freeze frame

C43

The pictures show something dangerous which might take place. In the empty space next to the picture, draw or write what happens next to prevent the danger.

Safety signs

Match the correct title to the safety sign.

- Caution, risk of explosion
- Risk of danger
- Caution, toxic/poison
- Eye protection must be worn
- Caution, risk of fire
- No smoking
- Not drinking water
- Caution, risk of danger

Safety designs

- Signs that say you must not do something are **circular** with a **red** border and cross bar. The background is in **white** with a centrally placed symbol in **black**.
- Warning signs are **triangular** with a **black** border. The background is **yellow** with a centrally placed symbol in **black**.
- Signs that say you must do something are **circular** with a **blue** background. There is a centrally placed symbol in **white**.

Design your own safety signs, using the proper colours.

What would I do?

What would you do if ...	
you cut your finger? 	
your brother had a nose bleed? 	
your Mum spilt boiling water on her hand? 	
your sister had grit in her eye? 	
your friend fell and cut themself badly on a piece of broken glass? 	
your cousin fell off a bike and you think they have broken their leg? 	
your Gran had fallen and banged her head and is unconscious? 	
you were first at an accident and the person wasn't breathing? 	

Breathing

Cut up the sentences and rearrange them in the correct order.

Our blood is pumped around our bodies by our hearts.

The cells in our bodies use the oxygen which has been transported by the blood replacing it with carbon dioxide.

Oxygen is in the air we breathe in through our mouth and nose.

In the lungs the oxygen goes into the blood.

Our breathing is controlled by our brain which needs oxygen to keep our bodies functioning.

It goes down the wind pipe or trachea into the lungs.

Cells in our bodies need oxygen to stay healthy.

When we breathe out the carbon dioxide is replaced by more oxygen as we breathe in.

Mouth to mouth

First check that nothing is blocking the airway. Loosen clothing around the neck. (For elderly people make sure you remove false teeth!)	
Open the airway by placing one hand under the person's neck, the other on the forehead, and tilt the head back.	
Move your hand from under the neck to the jaw and push up. This will open up the airway properly.	
Take a deep breath, pinch the person's nostrils together and place your lips around the person's mouth.	
Blow firmly until the person's chest rises. Take your mouth away. Breathe in as the chest falls.	
Do this three or four times fairly quickly and then repeat the process about every fifteen seconds.	
Keep doing this until the person starts breathing again or an adult can take over from you. Never give up. People can often recover a long time afterwards.	
When the person begins breathing again, place them in the recovery position.	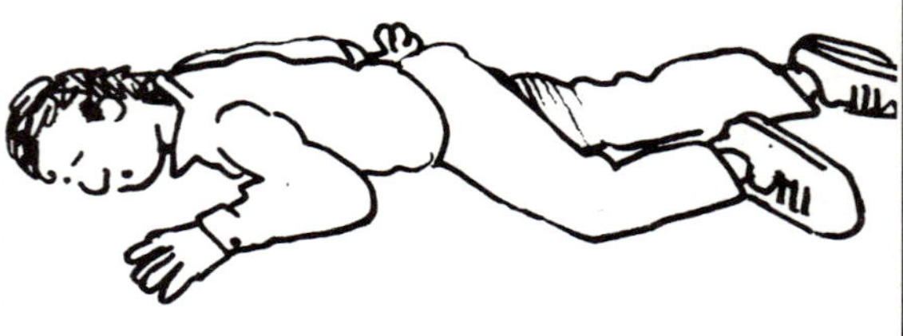

The circulation game

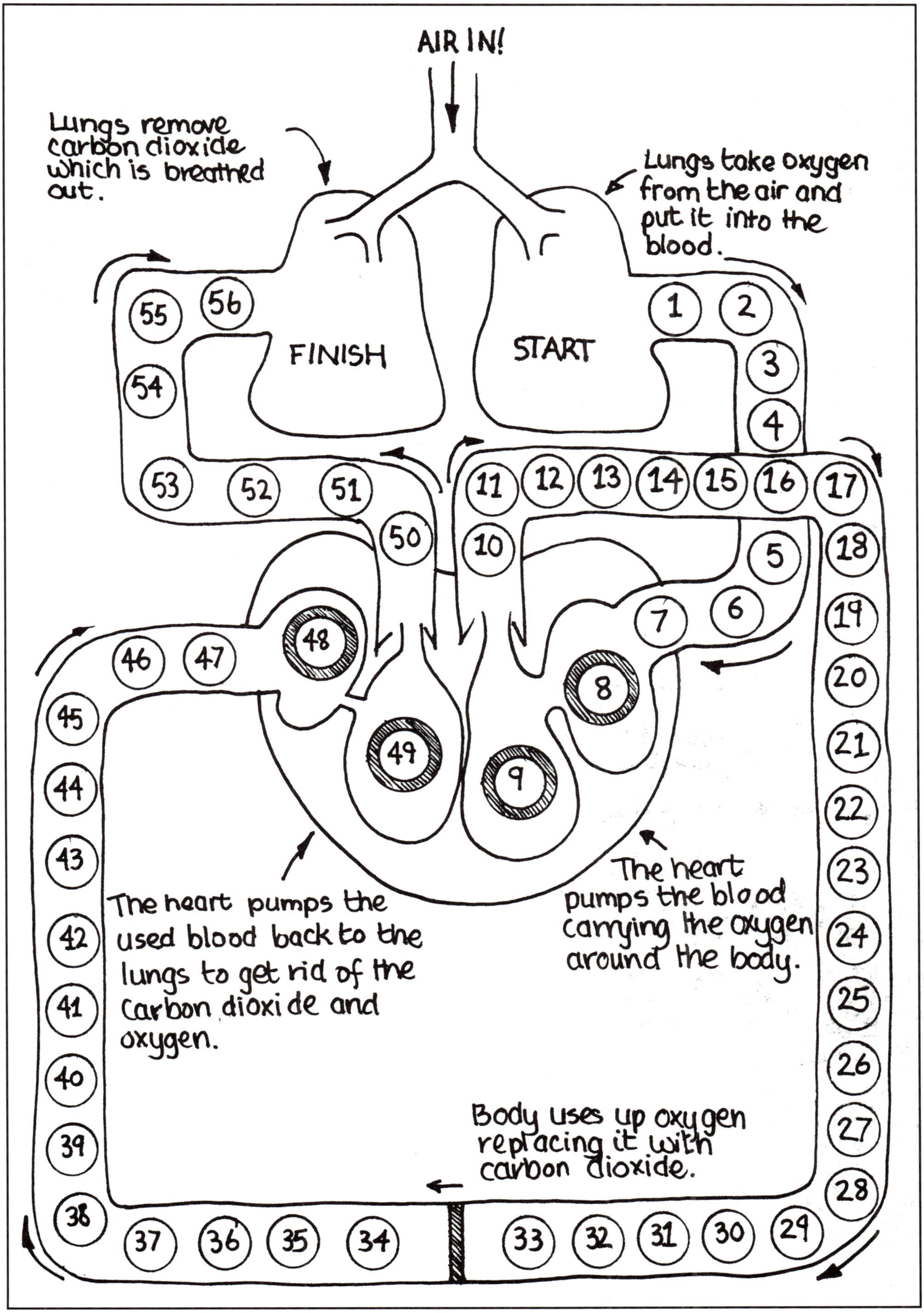

Unsafe environments

Area	Potential danger

Rules for being safe

Protected!

Match the activity to the correct protective equipment.

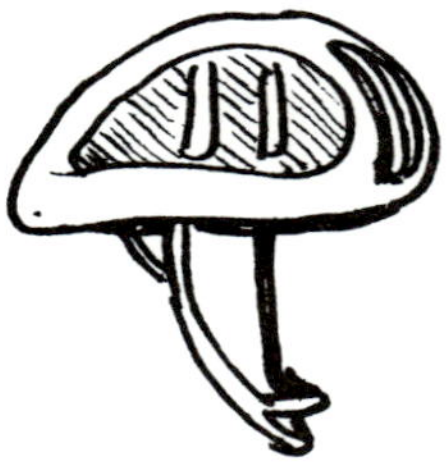

Car template

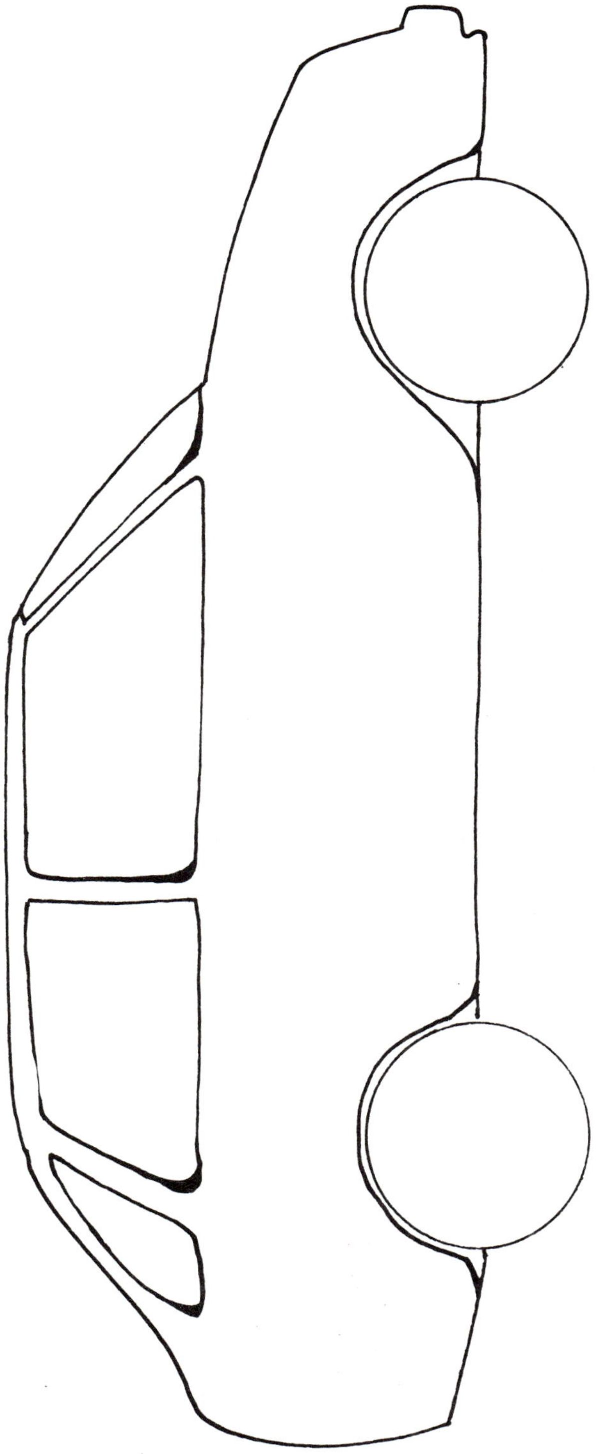

Stopping distances

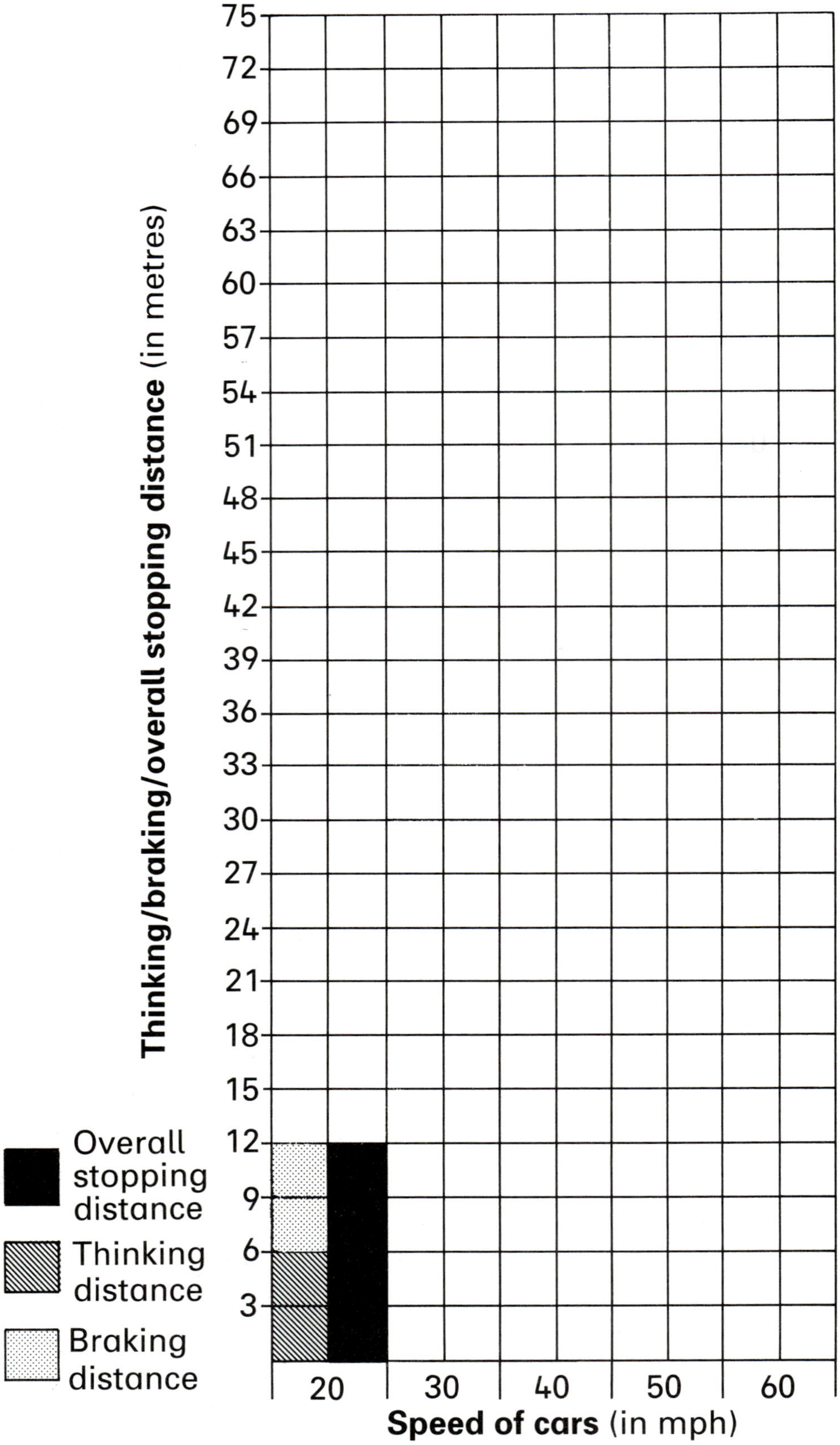

Festivals (1)

The Sikh festival of Baisakhi

This festival is the celebration of the Sikh creation of the Khalsa (Sikh self-identity, stressing love of God, equality and care for all regardless of race, class or religion) and receiving the 'Five Ks'.

At a meeting held in 1699, Guru Gobind Rai decided to test his followers. Standing before a crowd, his sword in his hand, he asked who would die for his faith. In turn he took five brave men into his tent and each time returned alone in front of the crowd with his sword dripping with blood. The crowd was terrified until he returned with the five brave men alive. Each man received from the guru five things each beginning with 'K' which served as a reminder to them to help them live a caring and honest life.

The Hindu festival of Divali

This festival celebrates the triumph of good over evil, the settling of old scores and the making of a new start.

King Rama and his wife Sita, were sent into the forest by their enemies, where they had to live in exile. One day Ravana, the ten-headed demon, kidnapped Sita and carried her off to his kingdom in Lanka. With the help of Hanuman, the monkey god, and Lakshmana, Rama's brother, King Rama traced his wife. Following a great battle, greatly assisted by Hanuman's army of monkeys, king Rama killed Ravana and rescued his wife. After this they returned to their kingdom and the throne that was rightfully his.

Festivals (2)

The Muslim festival of Eid ul-Adha

Submission to the will of Allah is usually what the term 'Islam' means. The story of Abraham and his son Isma'ail is a strong reminder of how Allah provides and looks after those who do his will.

The great prophet Abraham had a son called Isma'ail who he loved very much. One night Abraham had a dream in which he was commanded to sacrifice his son as an offering to Allah. Waking from his troubled dream he told Isma'ail what he had been asked to do. Immediately Isma'ail offered himself to his father. Just as Abraham was about to raise his knife, the voice of Allah spoke to him telling him not to harm the boy. What had taken place had only been a test.

Nearby, a goat had been placed by Allah and this was killed in place of Isma'ail.

The Christian festival of Easter

For Christians throughout the world, the celebration of Easter marks the crucifixion of Jesus Christ and his resurrection from the dead.

In the country known as Palestine, Jesus acquired a large following of people who listened to his preaching and watched his healing with awe and admiration. The Roman rulers and Jewish authorities were alarmed at the influence Jesus had over the people and wondered how to get rid of him. By bribing Judas, a friend and follower of Jesus, they were able to find out where Jesus was. They arrested him and shortly after condemned him to die by being nailed to a cross. Although in great pain, Jesus suffered bravely and forgave those who had been his enemies, for he knew that he would be reunited with God.

Talking heads

Something I know about being safe by the road is

____

____

______________________________________.

Something I know about being safe near railway tracks is

____

____

______________________________________.

Something I know about being safe by the canal is

____

____

______________________________________.

Something I know about being safe when playing by myself is

____

____

______________________________________.

Something I know about being safe in school is

____

____

______________________________________.

Five things I know about exercise

My personal exercise diary

Name ______________________________ Class ______________

Day	Physical activity I took part in	Duration	How it made me feel
Monday			
Tuesday			
Wednesday			
Thursday			
Friday			
Saturday			
Sunday			
The activity I enjoyed most was		Total hours: mins	Signed parent/guardian

Stamina, suppleness and strength

Choose some sporting activities and assess them for stamina, suppleness and strength.

Levels: very much (✓✓✓) some extent (✓✓) not much (✓)

Sporting activity	Stamina	Suppleness	Strength

Sport and the 3 S's

Sporting activity	Stamina	Suppleness	Strength
football	✓✓✓	✓✓✓	✓✓✓
cricket	✓	✓✓	✓
cycling	✓✓✓	✓✓	✓✓✓
golf	✓	✓✓	✓
gymnastics	✓✓	✓✓✓	✓✓✓
jogging	✓✓✓	✓✓	✓✓
swimming	✓✓✓	✓✓✓	✓✓✓
sailing	✓	✓✓	✓✓
tennis	✓✓	✓✓✓	✓✓
badminton	✓✓	✓✓✓	✓✓
judo	✓✓	✓✓✓	✓✓

Levels: very much (✓✓✓) some extent (✓✓) not much (✓)

Write as many words as you can think of that describe the type of movements and facial expressions likely to be shown by a sportsman or woman of a sport you have chosen to report on.

Getting back to fitness

Physical activity	Stamina	Suppleness	Strength
Housework	✓	✓✓	✓
Gardening (digging)	✓✓✓	✓✓	✓✓✓
Walking (fast)	✓✓✓	✓	✓✓
Dancing (disco)	✓✓	✓✓✓	✓
Dancing (ballroom)	✓	✓✓	✓
Mowing lawn	✓✓	✓	✓✓✓
Climbing stairs	✓✓✓	✓	✓✓

Expert advice

1) A young girl aged ten who has had no exercise for six months because of a broken leg which has just come out of plaster.	**Recommendation**
2) An old age pensioner worried about her health having just recovered from a mild heart attack.	**Recommendation**
3) A young mother who has just had a baby and wants to recover her fitness.	**Recommendation**

Toning up

Cut out the picture on the right. Mount it on to a piece of card and then cut out each piece. Following an exercise on the left of the page, copy it by arranging the pieces in the position of the exercise. You may have to trim your pieces a little in order to get the position right. Afterwards, you may use your figure to make up some of your own exercise positions.

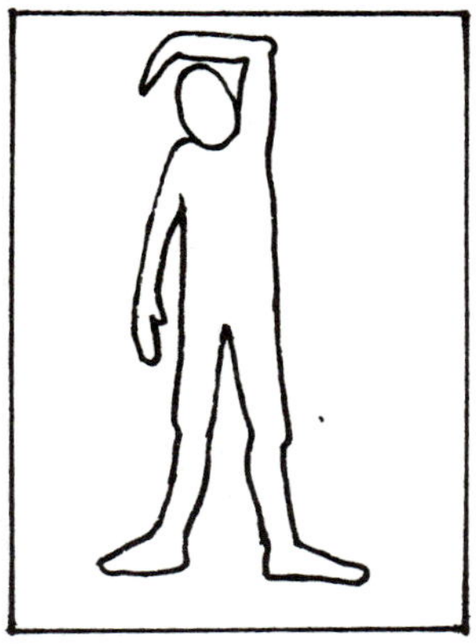

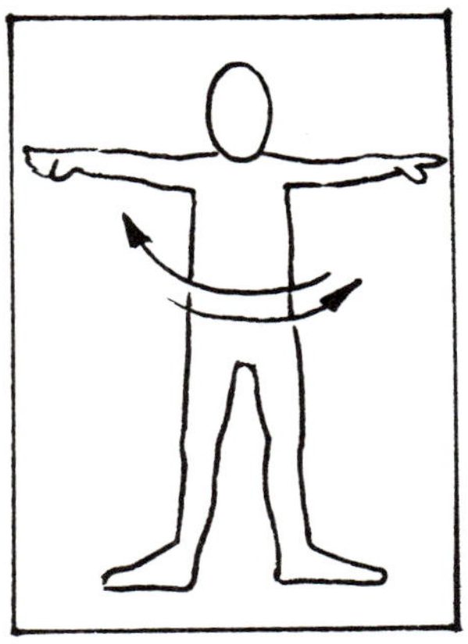

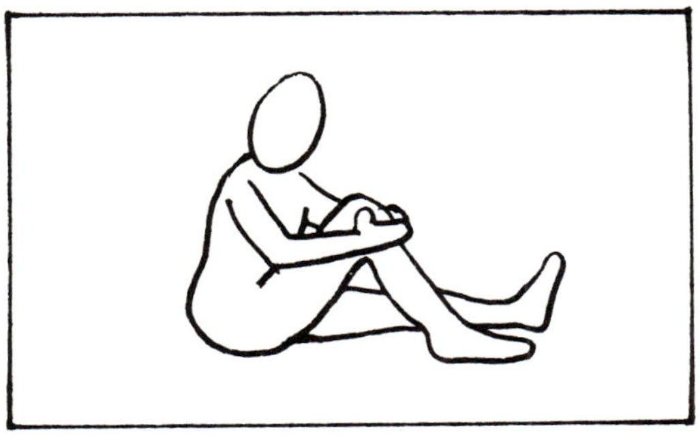

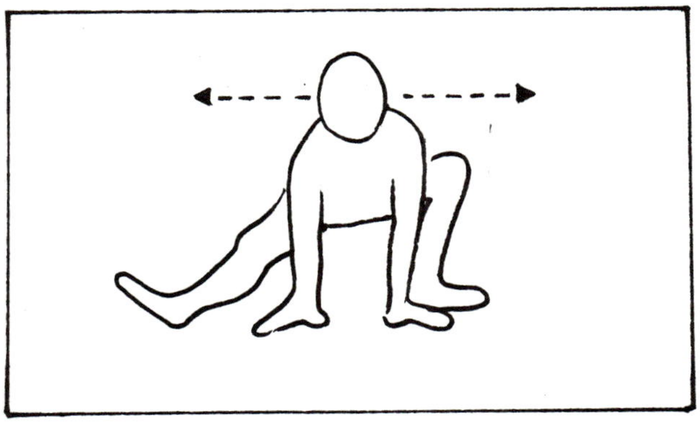

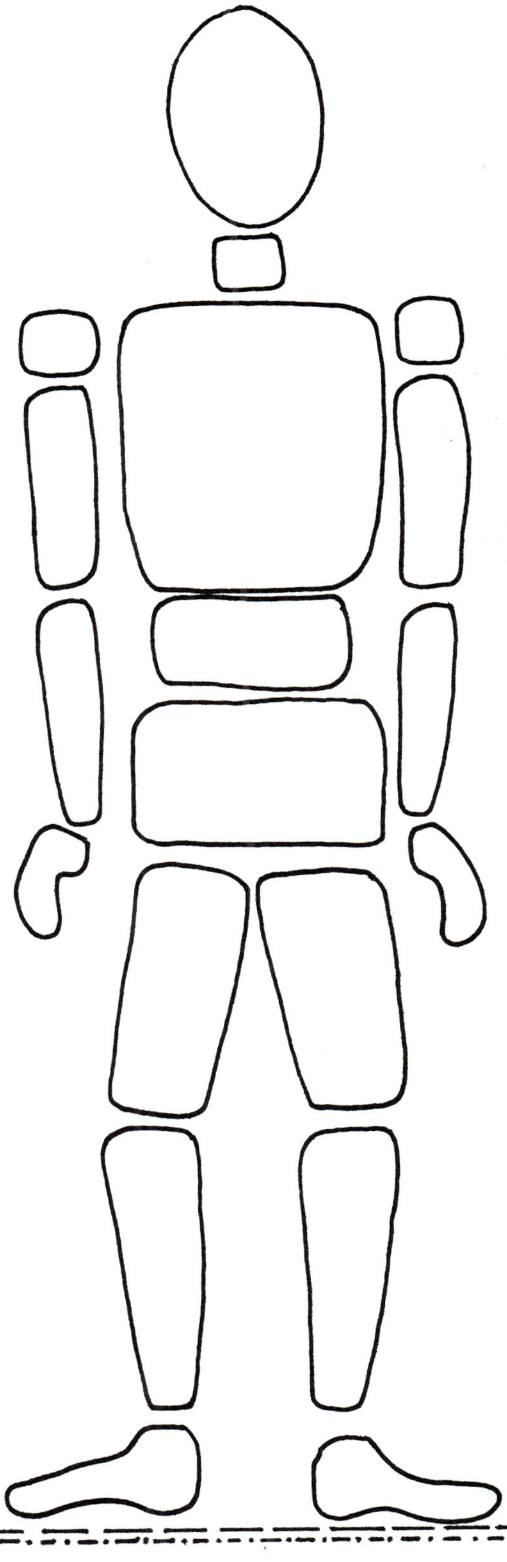

Ten amazing facts

Place the correct number in the blank space for each statement, once you have checked its accuracy.

1) There are about _____ muscles in the human body.

2) Our skeletons have over _____ moving joints.

3) There are over _____ kms of blood vessels in our bodies.

4) Each adult has _____ bones, most of them being in the hands and feet.

5) Human bone is very strong. A block of bone the size of 3 cm^2 can support _____ tonnes weight.

6) Our hearts will beat over _____ million times in our life span.

7) The body's entire blood supply of _____ l washes through the lungs once a minute.

8) The heart creates enough power every day to lift an average size car _____ m off the ground.

9) The body of an average adult contains _____ l of water which is about 65 percent of his/her weight.

10) Our bodies contain enough calcium to make a box of chalk: enough carbon to make a _____ kg bag of coke and phosphorus to make 2,200 match heads.

Source: *Reader's Digest Book of Facts*, 1985

Pulse rates

My pulse rate for 1 minute is ________ (a).

My pulse rate for 1 hour is:
(a) ________ × 60 minutes = ________ (b).

My pulse rate for 1 day is:
(b) ________ × 24 hours = ________ (c).

My pulse rate for 1 week is:
(c) ________ × 7 days = ________ (d).

My pulse rate for 1 year is:
(d) ________ × 52 weeks = ________ (e).

If I live to the age of 70 my heart will have beaten:

(e) ________ × 70 years = ________ (f).

Total number of heart beats in 70 years

= ________ (f).

How tall will I be?

My present height is ________ cm.

Percentage of full height at:

Age	Boys (percentage)	Girls (percentage)
8	72	77.5
9	75	80.5
10	78	84.5
11	81	88.5
12	84	93.0

Formula

$$\frac{\text{My present height in cm}}{\text{\% of full height}} \times \frac{100}{1}$$

Example

A girl aged 10 who is 135 cm tall.

$$\frac{135}{84.5} \times \frac{100}{1} = 159.7\text{ cm.}$$

Your turn

$$\frac{\text{Height}}{\%} \times \frac{100}{1} =$$

I am likely to be ______ cm tall as an adult.

Sporting history

Match the sport to the date when it was first introduced.

Choose from the following dates: 600 BC, 1800s, 1830s, 1700s, 1600s, 1500s, 1400s, 1500s.

tennis

skiing

athletics

football

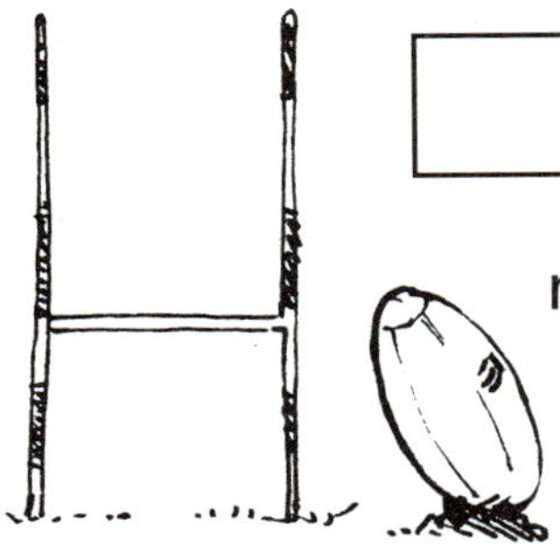

rugby

golf

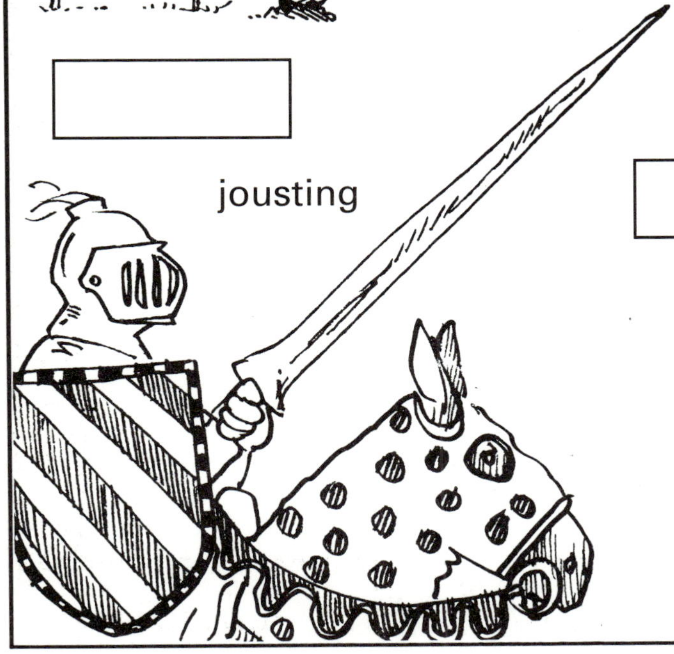

jousting

squash

Ancient sports

Sports and pastimes of the Middle Ages

Colour the border around those sports or pastimes still being played today. Tick in the box those activities which require no equipment and tick in the circle those activities that are very active and therefore good exercise for the body.

archery ○ ☐

jumping ○ ☐

wrestling ○ ☐

dancing ○ ☐

hunting ○ ☐

bear baiting ○ ☐

football ○ ☐

jousting ○ ☐

running ○ ☐

throwing ○ ☐

bull baiting ○ ☐

mock battles ○ ☐

Olympiads (1)

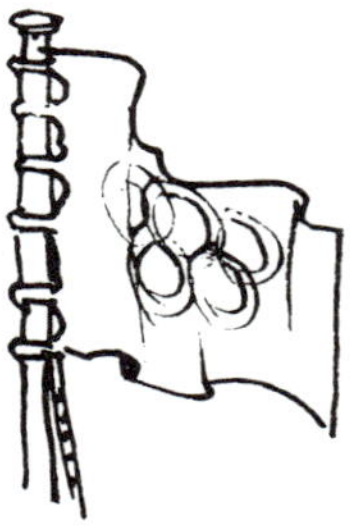

Date	City	Host country
1896	Athens	
1900	Paris	
1904	St Louis	
1908	London	
1912	Stockholm	
1920	Antwerp	
1924	Paris	
1928	Amsterdam	
1932	Los Angeles	
1936	Berlin	
1948	London	
1952	Helsinki	
1956	Melbourne	
1960	Rome	
1964	Tokyo	
1968	Mexico City	
1972	Munich	
1976	Montreal	
1980	Moscow	
1984	Los Angeles	
1988	Seoul	
1992	Barcelona	
1996		
2000		
2004		

Olympiads (2)

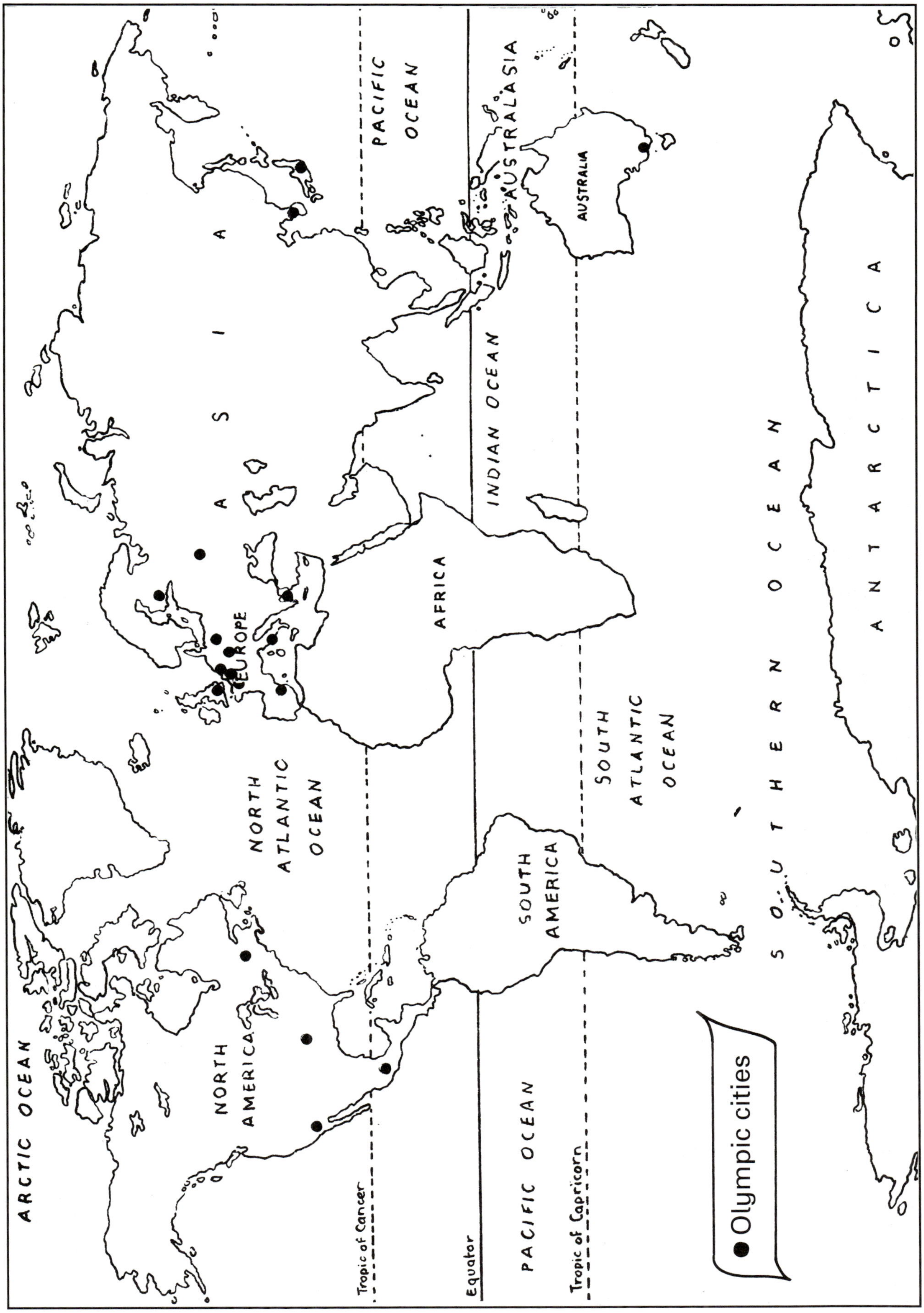
ARCTIC OCEAN
NORTH AMERICA
Tropic of Cancer
Equator
PACIFIC OCEAN
Tropic of Capricorn
NORTH ATLANTIC OCEAN
SOUTH AMERICA
SOUTH ATLANTIC OCEAN
EUROPE
AFRICA
ASIA
PACIFIC OCEAN
INDIAN OCEAN
AUSTRALASIA
AUSTRALIA
SOUTHERN OCEAN
ANTARCTICA
Olympic cities

Personal bests

My pulse rate standing still is ________________.

My pulse rate after exercise is ________________.

My personal bests for exercising

Activity	Day 1	Day 2	Day 3	Day 4	Total time	Average
60 metres dash						
obstacle course						
ball control						
hopping						
running backwards						

The activity I improved most was ________________.

My best average time was ________________.

The activity I enjoyed most was ________________.

My 'PB's

I can ____

____

____

____.

I would like to ____

____

____

____.

I am good at ____

____

____

____.

I am going to ____

____

____

____.

I would like to be better at ______________________

____.

I will tell ____

when I have been successful.

People and places

Place the words in the middle box into the group where each belongs.

People who worship

Places where people worship

athletes, temple, mosque, believers, studio, church, captain, synagogue, rabbi, meeting house, gurudwara, mullah, followers, priest, swimming pool, competitors, stadium, instructor, imam, congregation, team, pastor, worshippers, guru, swami, track, parishioners, father, bishop, players, dancers

People who take part in sport

Places where people take part in sport

The skeleton

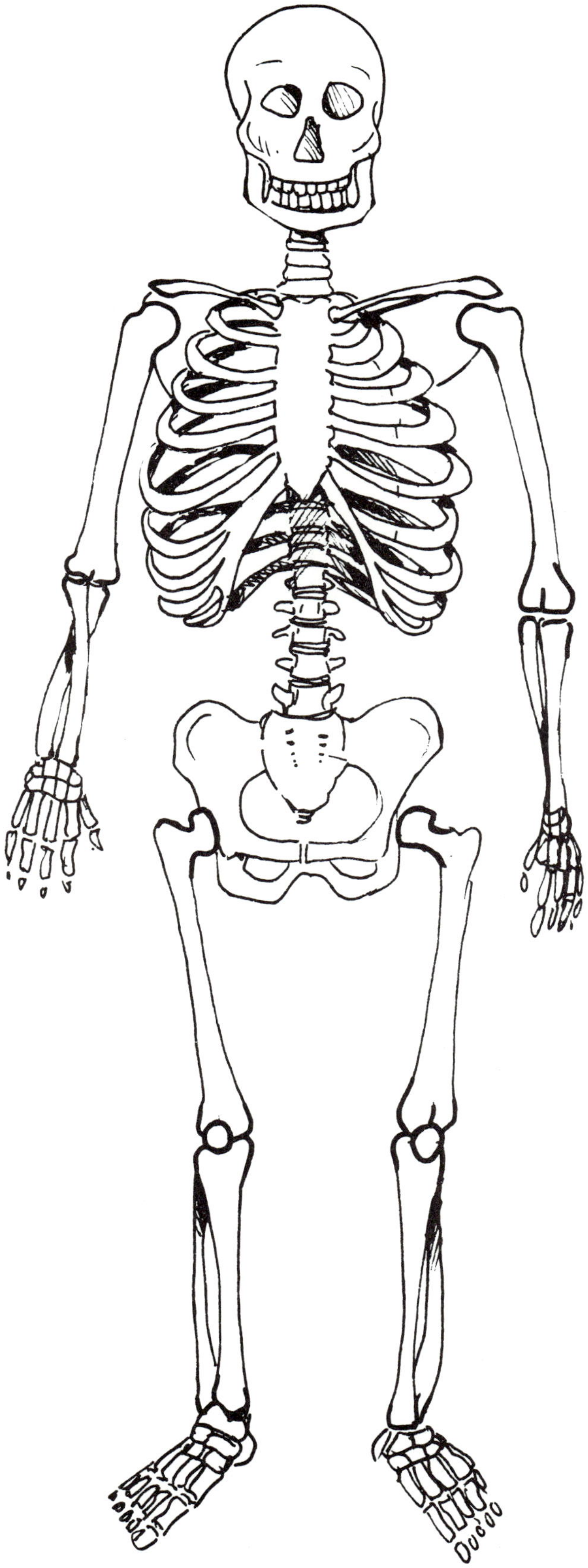

Joints and movement

What type of joint is the part of the skeleton shown in each of the pictures? State what kind of movement each joint will allow.

Part of the skeleton	Type of joint and movement
hip 	
elbow 	
ankle 	
shoulder 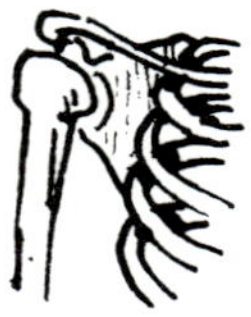	
fingers 	
toes 	
knees 	

My food preferences

Food choice	Why I like this food	Healthy ☺ Unhealthy ☹

I think that my diet is ____________________________________.

My digestion

C78

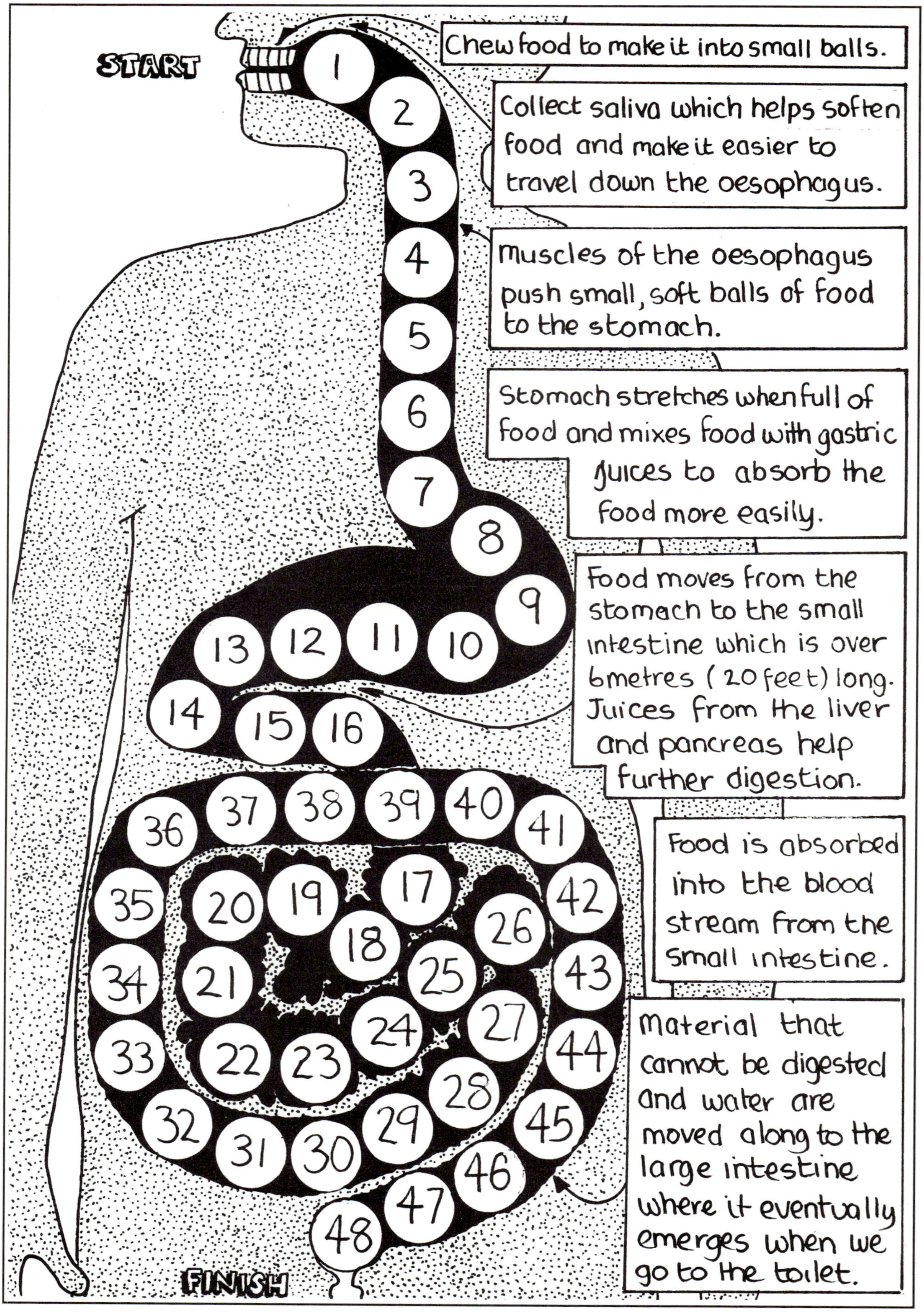

Food groups

Foods containing protein	Foods containing carbohydrates	Foods containing vitamins and minerals

Nutrition labels

Food product (per serving)	Energy	Protein	Carbohydrate	Sugar	Fibre	Fat	Salt	Vitamins and minerals
e.g. Cornflakes	750kg	7gm	32gm	9gm	0·7gm	0·4gm	0·2gm	160mg

Changing me

Something I would like to change about me is ...

Write your thoughts around the picture. You don't have to change anything at all if you don't want to.

Weighing up

Hyacinth does not want the cream cakes her Mum has brought home for tea. Hyacinth is worried that she is putting on weight. How can she refuse them and explain to her Mum that she wants foods that have less sugar and fat in them?

Leroy is bigger than his classmates and he is not very good at games. Because of this he is teased and sometimes called names by other children. You are his friends and don't think this is very fair.

Richard's parents are both at work so Richard has to stay for school dinners. He doesn't like them so he spends his dinner money on chocolate and cakes before school. You are his best friends and are worried about this.

Amjad will not eat anything but chips and crisps. He will not eat his Mum's cooking, saying that all his friends eat chips. What can Amjad's Mum do?

Your school tuck shop sells only biscuits and crisps. Danielle and her friends feel that the tuck shop should sell healthy snacks too. How can they bring this about?

Calorie count

Product	Weight (g)	Fat (g)	Carbohydrate (g)	Protein (g)	Calories
Dairy					
Cow's milk	244	9	12	2	160
Cheese (cheddar)	28	9	0.6	7	115
Cheese (cottage)	200	1	5.4	34	117
Cream	15	3	0.6	1	30
Fish					
Fish fingers	112	10	8	19	200
Cod (grilled)	100	5	0	12	170
Sardines	85	9	0	22	180
Tuna	85	7	0	25	170
Fruit					
Banana	150	trace	23	1	85
Apple	250	0	34	trace	125
Pear	182	1	21.8	1	100
Orange	180	trace	16	2	60
Vegetables					
Potato chips	60	7	20	1	155
Carrots (raw)	110	trace	10	1	45
Cabbage	170	trace	9	2	45
Lettuce	100	trace	2	1	14
Meat/poultry					
Roast beef	85	36	0	16	390
Chicken (fried)	85	15	0	25	245
Lamb (roast)	85	14	0	20	314
Oils/fats					
Butter	112	90	1	trace	800
Margarine	112	90	trace	trace	805
Bread/cereals					
Brown (slice)	28	1	11	3	65
Cornflakes	25	trace	25	2	110
Pizza (slice)	75	6	23	8	180
Shredded wheat	28	1	23	3	100
Beverages					
Coffee	230	0	1	trace	3
Tea	230	trace	1	0	4
Lemonade	346	0	38	0	137
Eggs					
Poached/boiled	50	6	trace	6	75
Fried	65	8	0.5	6.5	110

A balanced diet

Boy	Girl	Age	Target calories
(place a tick in the appropriate box)			(state number of calories per day)

DIET FOR THE DAY

Breakfast

Total calories

Lunch

Total calories

Dinner

Total calories

Snacks

Total calories

Ministry of Food

The number of calories needed each day for children (according to age and average weight and height)

Age	Calories
1–3 years	1,300
3–6 years	1,600
6–9 years	2,100
9–12 years (girl)	2,200
9–12 years (boy)	2,400

1 For body-building

Some fillings and stuffings

MEAT, CHEESE, FISH, CANNED PILCHARDS, CANNED PINK SALMON. Season, sometimes add a dash of sauce, and mash.

DRIED BEANS OR PEAS. Soak 12–24 hours and cook, then mash and mix with grated cheese or household milk, flavour with meat or with vegetable or meat extract. Canned beans in brine are already cooked and cost no points.

DRIED EGG. Mix in usual way, put in a greased basin, cook in a saucepan of boiling water for 15 minutes. Turn out and chop.

2 For energy

BUTTER, MARGARINE, DRIPPING.

BAKED POTATOES. Choose firm ones, cook in skins, peel, split (or if very large slice thickly) and use as covers for sandwiches.

POTATO PASTRY. Use for turnovers or cut into squares for sandwiches – jam, fruit or savoury.

HOME-MADE POTATO SCONES.

BREAD, FLOUR. But please be sparing with both, to save shipping space.

3 For protection

A SALAD. Shredded raw vegetables with a little seasoning and dressing or vinegar.

A BUNCH OF WATERCRESS.

A FEW NEW TURNIPS PEELED: SOME YOUNG CARROTS. MUSTARD AND CRESS.

COARSELY CHOPPED PARSLEY, CHOPPED GREEN TOPS OF SPRING ONIONS to sprinkle in sandwiches.

FRUIT when in season.

1) For body-building

2) For energy

3) For protection

Source: Ministry of food, 1943

Good for growing

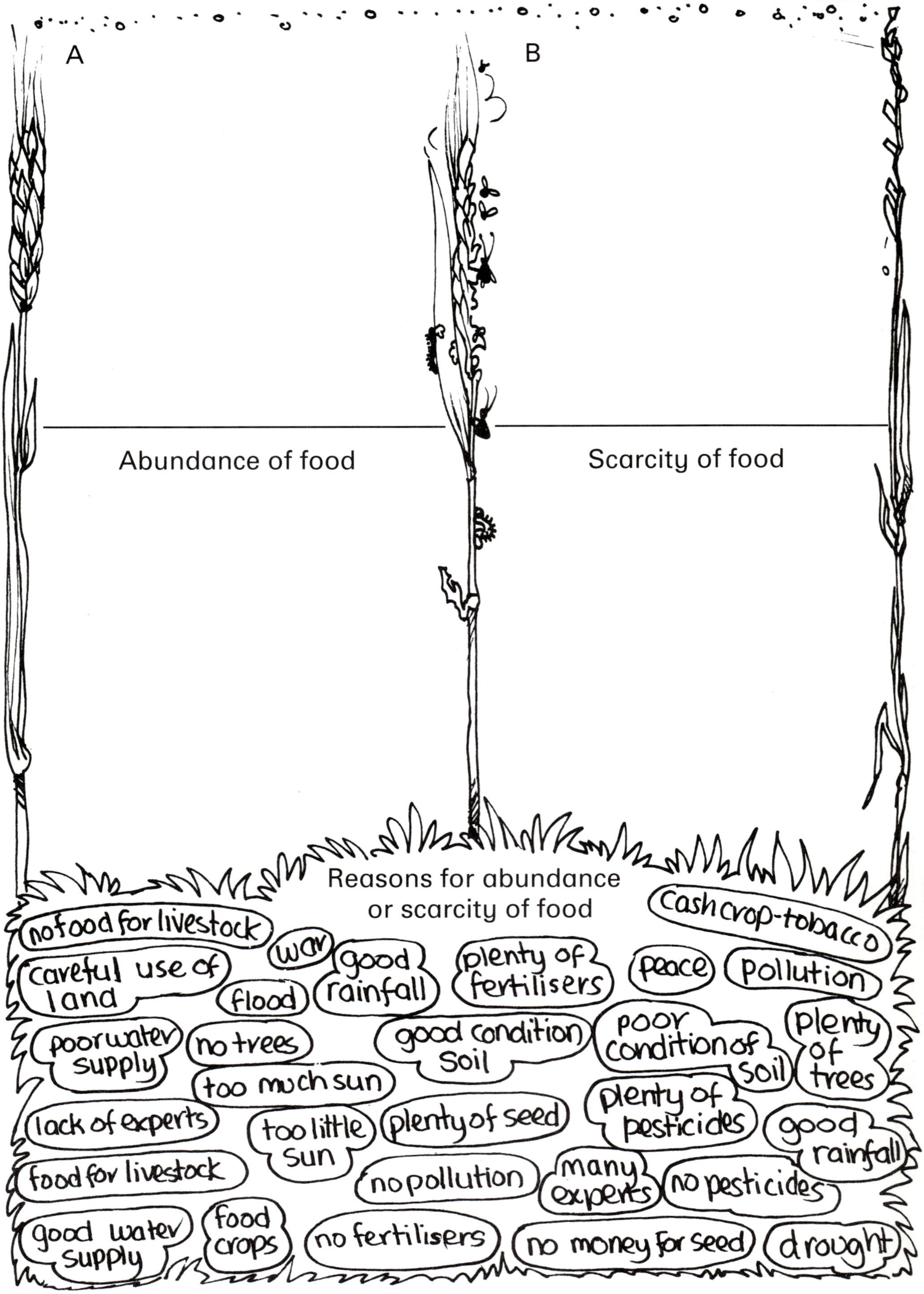

World food map

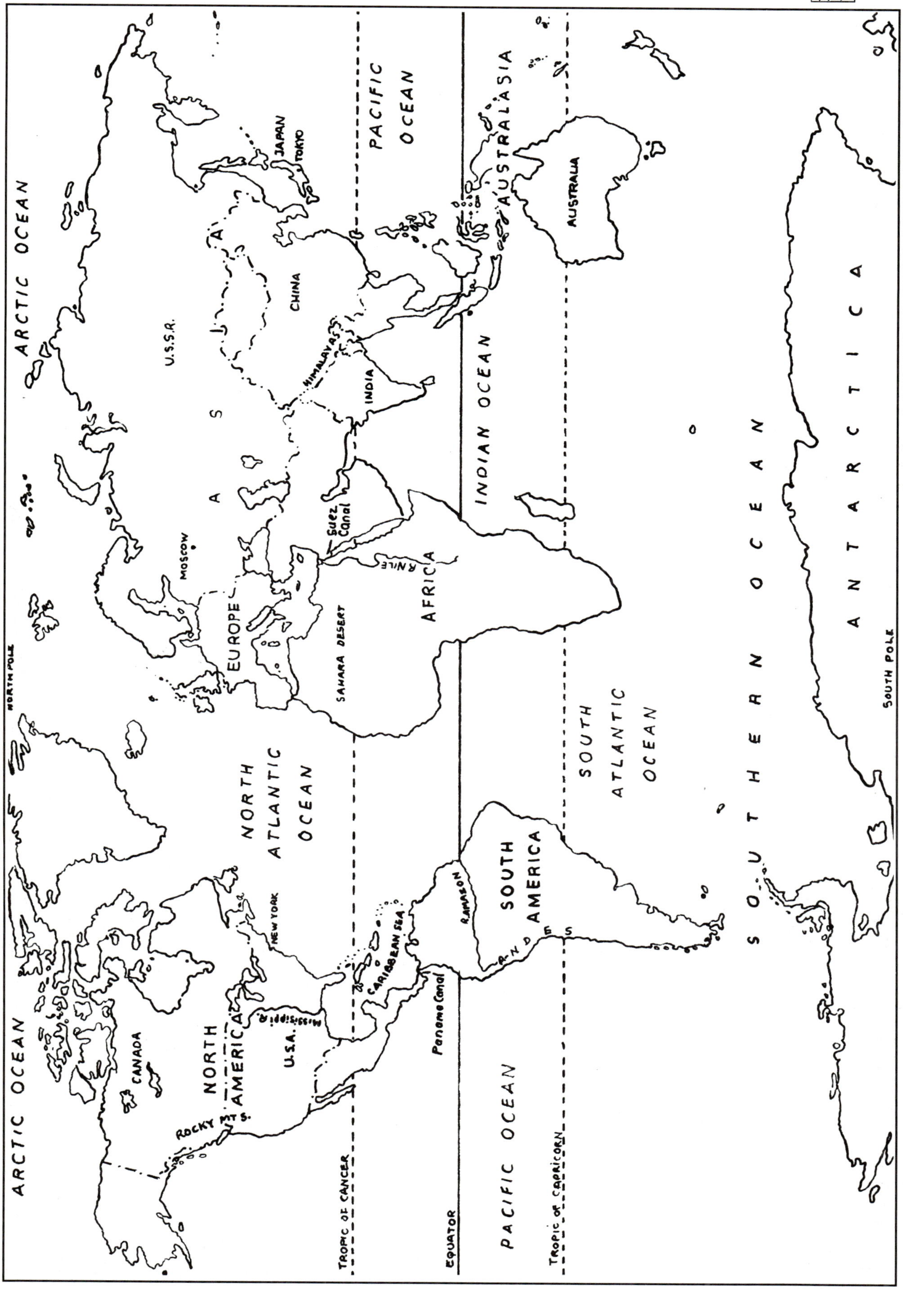

Counting crafty calories

Counting crafty calories creeping up on me,
Full of vital vitamins, A, B and C.
Providing lots of proteins for building up my body,
But not to watch those calories will leave me feeling
sorry.

Chorus
So let's eat healthily and take lots of exercise,
A proper balanced diet and you'll stay a proper size.
Don't take toxins – give your lungs a rest,
You won't eat your heart out – but lead of life of zest!

Fend off fatty food; cream, cheese and butter
Eyeing carbohydrates, mainly starch and sugars.
Managing the minerals mooching in my blood,
Vying with the vitamins to do my bones some good.

Chorus
So let's eat healthily and take lots of exercise,
A proper balanced diet and you'll stay a proper size.
Don't take toxins – give your lungs a rest,
You won't eat your heart out – but lead a life of zest!

Ron Morton

Foods and festivals

Food	Religion	Festival	When
Fruit			
bananas	Hindu	Rama Naumi	April
melon	Chinese	Moon Festival	September
tangerines	Chinese	New Year	January/ February
Vegetables			
aubergines	Sikh	Guru Nanak's birthday	November
horseradish	Jewish	Passover	March/April
rice	Hindu	Death rites	
Cakes/pastry			
bread	Christian	Harvest	September
dumplings	Chinese	Dragon Boat	June
chapatis	Sikh	Baisakhi	April
hamen-tashen	Jewish	Purim	February/March
moon cakes	Chinese	Moon Festival	September
noodles	Buddhist	Dhammacakka	July
Meat/poultry			
lamb	Muslim	Eid ul-Adha	March/April
goat	Muslim	Birth rites	
turkey	Christian	Christmas	December

Shopping list for festivals

Food colourings

See how many food colourings you can find by looking carefully at various food labels in your larder and refrigerator at home or at those provided by your teacher.

Name of food colour	Colour	Food used in
Ponceau MX		
Ponceau 4R		
Carmoisine		
Amaranth		
Red 10B		
Erythrosine BS		
Red 2G		
Red 6b		
Fast red E		
Orange G		
Orange RN		
Oil yellow GG		
Tartrazine		
Yellow 2G		
Sunset yellow FCP		
Oil yellow GG		
Green S		
Indigo carmine		
Violet BNP		
Brown FK		
Chocolate brown FB		
Chocolate brown HT		
Black PN		
Black 7984		

Remembering healthy eating

C91

1) What do we need food for?

____

2) What do we need proteins for?

____

3) Three examples of protein foods are

(a) ______________ (b) ______________ (c) ______________

4) What do we need carbohydrates for?

____

5) Three examples of carbohydrate foods are

(a) ______________ (b) ______________ (c) ______________

6) Why do we need the mineral calcium in our food?

____

7) Why do we need plenty of vitamin C?

____

8) Where can (a) calcium and (b) vitamin C be found?

(a) ______________ (b) ______________

9) Why do we need foods with a lot of fibre in them?

____

10) Which foods should we eat less of?

____

11) Which foods should we eat more of?

____

12) What happens if we eat more calories than our bodies can use?

____

13) What two things can we do to ensure that we don't become overweight?

(a) ______________ (b) ______________

14) How can we find out what each food we eat contains?

____

My skin

Write a different function of your skin in each steam bubble.

Animal covers

	Covering	Environment
 crocodile		
 snake		
 elephant		
 fish		
 polar bear		
 bird		
 porcupine		

Bacterium

A

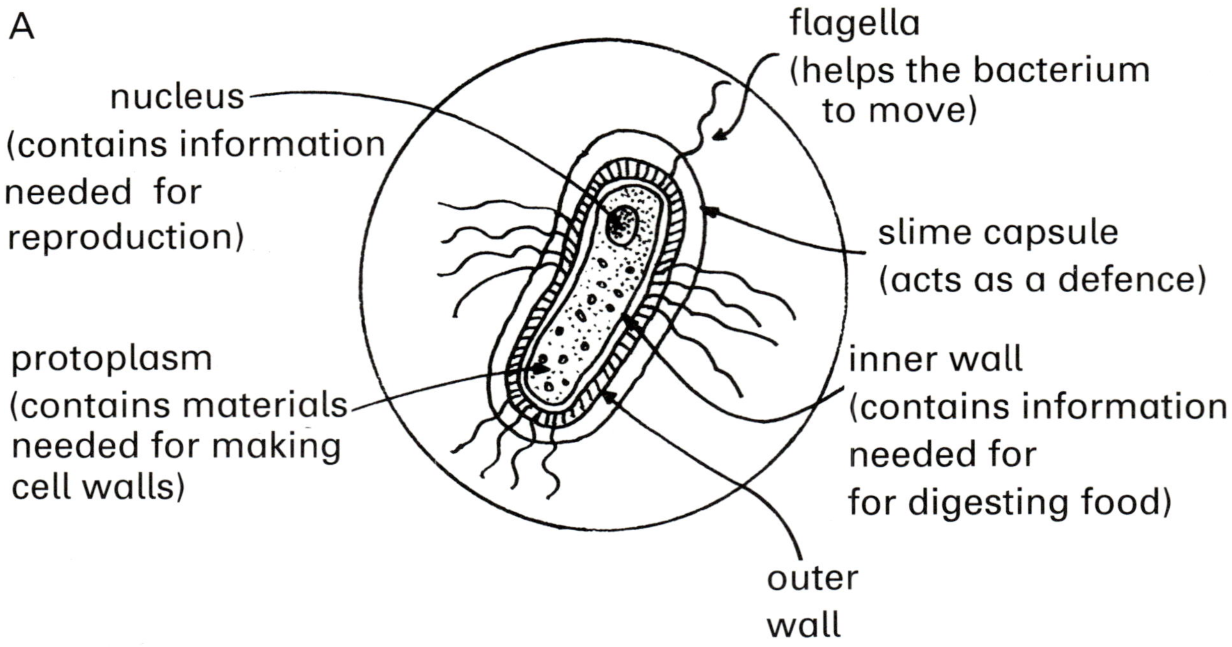

B

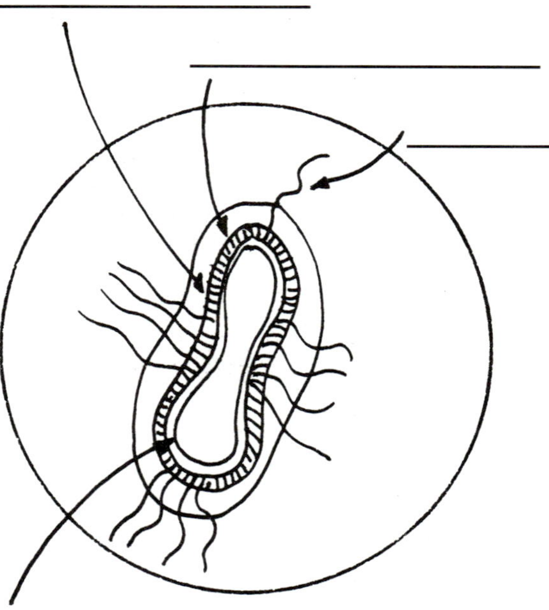

C

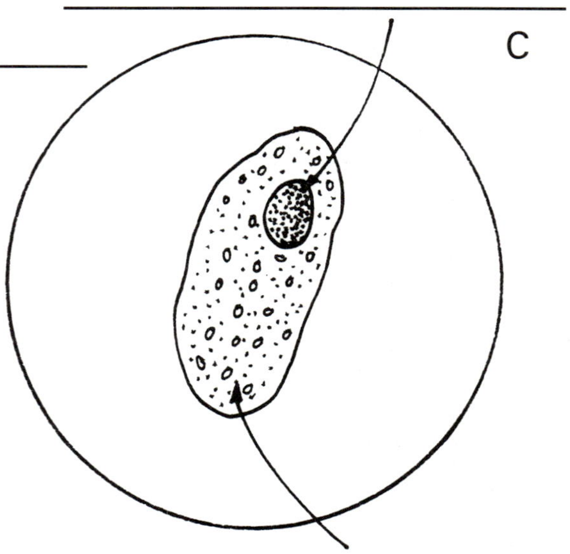

D

Now draw your own bacterium.

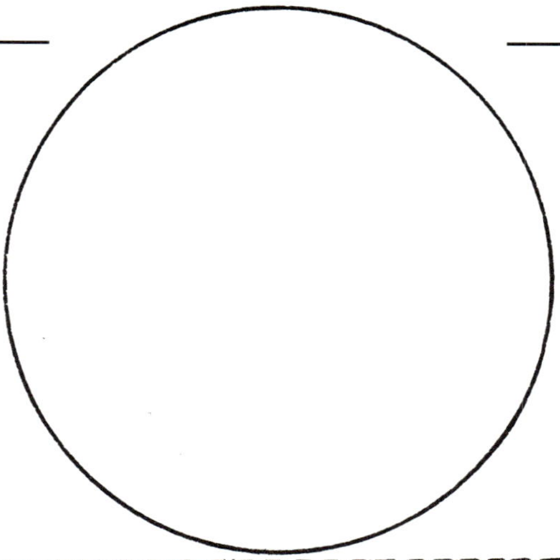

Brushing out bacteria

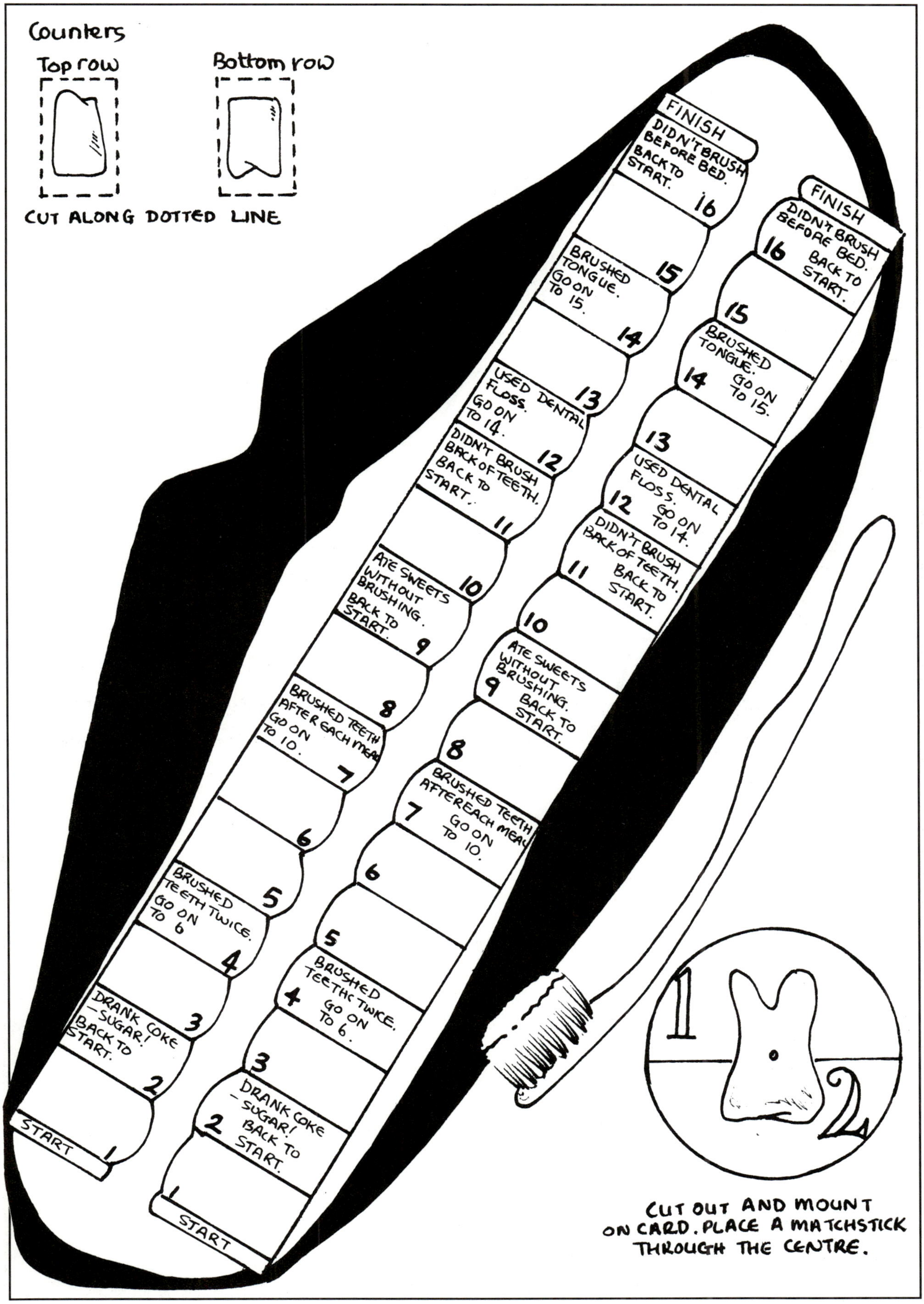

Teeth

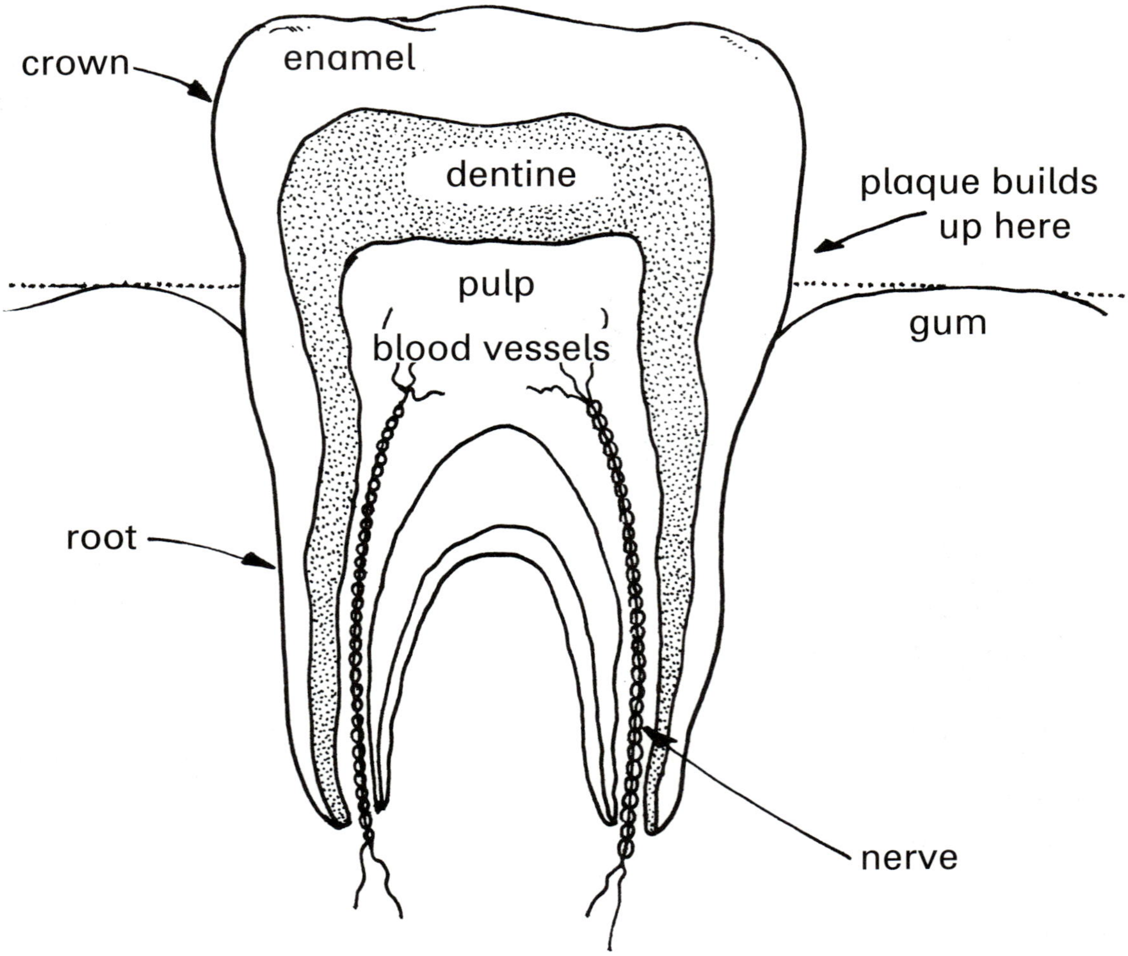

- Enamel is hard and protects the tooth from damage.
- Dentine is the heavy interior of the tooth.
- Pulp is the soft centre of the tooth supplied by blood and full of nerves.
- The crown is the part of the tooth above the gums.
- Plaque is the build up of food and bacteria on the tooth which allows acids to make holes in the enamel causing cavities. This also can cause gum disease which can be painful too.

Using water

A Record how often you do each of the following: take a bath, have a shower, brush your teeth, flush the toilet.

	Sun	Mon	Tue	Wed	Thu	Fri	Sat	**Total**

B Record the amount of water held by a school wash-basin, toilet cistern and sink. Then record how much water you think will be used by you during the day or week.

	Amount of water held	Amount used that day/week

C Say why it is important for people to wash themselves and their clothes regularly.

Purification

Write in each box those things that might be expected of Christians, Muslims and Hindus which show they are leading a good life according to their faith. In the circle, place all those things that are common to the three religions.

CHRISTIANITY

ISLAM

Leading a good life – things in common – Christianity, Islam and Hinduism.

HINDUISM

Clean water

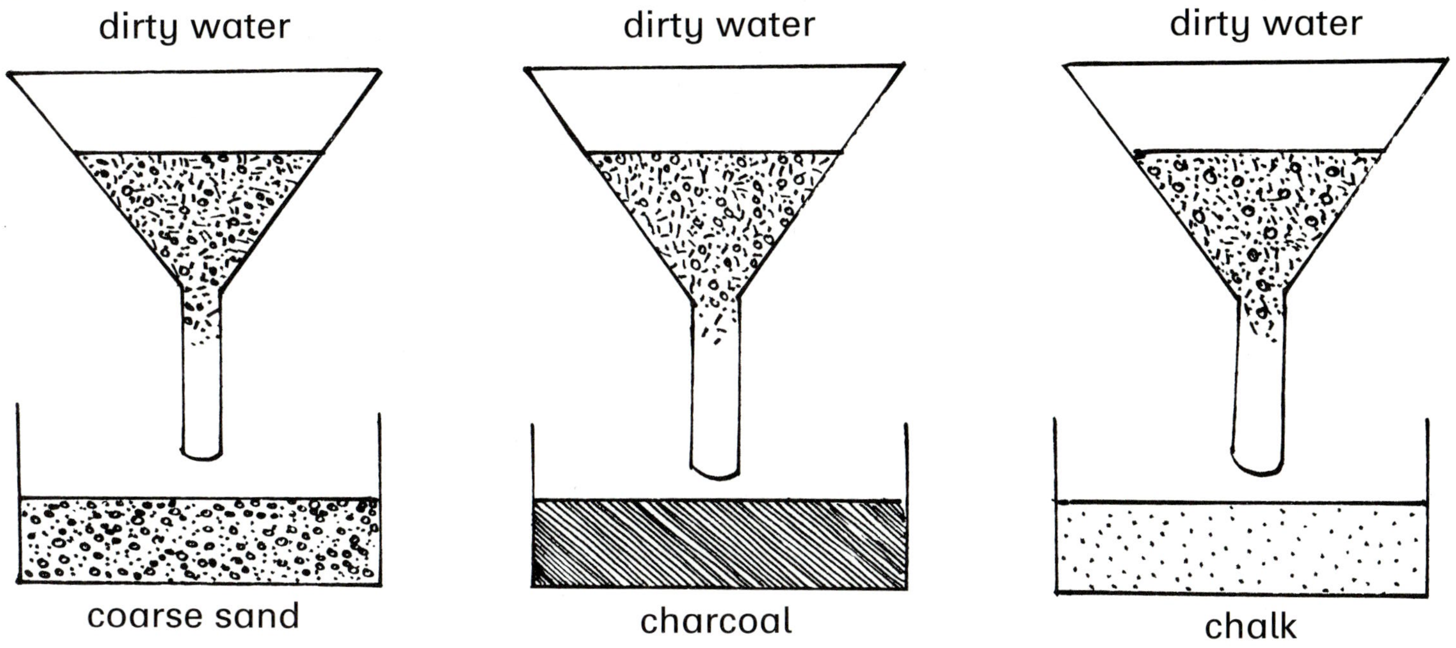

1) Pour a measured amount of dirty water into each funnel – which one do you think will work best?
2) Allow the water to pass through the filters – coarse sand, charcoal, chalk.
3) Remove the filters and compare the three samples of water.
4) Which is the 'cleanest'? Was it the one you predicted?
5) Now repeat the process for any other materials you may consider would make good/effective filters.
6) Write about what you did: how you did it, what you predicted, what you saw and what you can conclude from this activity.

Smelly bits

Mark the areas of the body requiring particular attention to cleanliness as we grow up. Use an arrow ➚ or a cross ✗ to show the area.

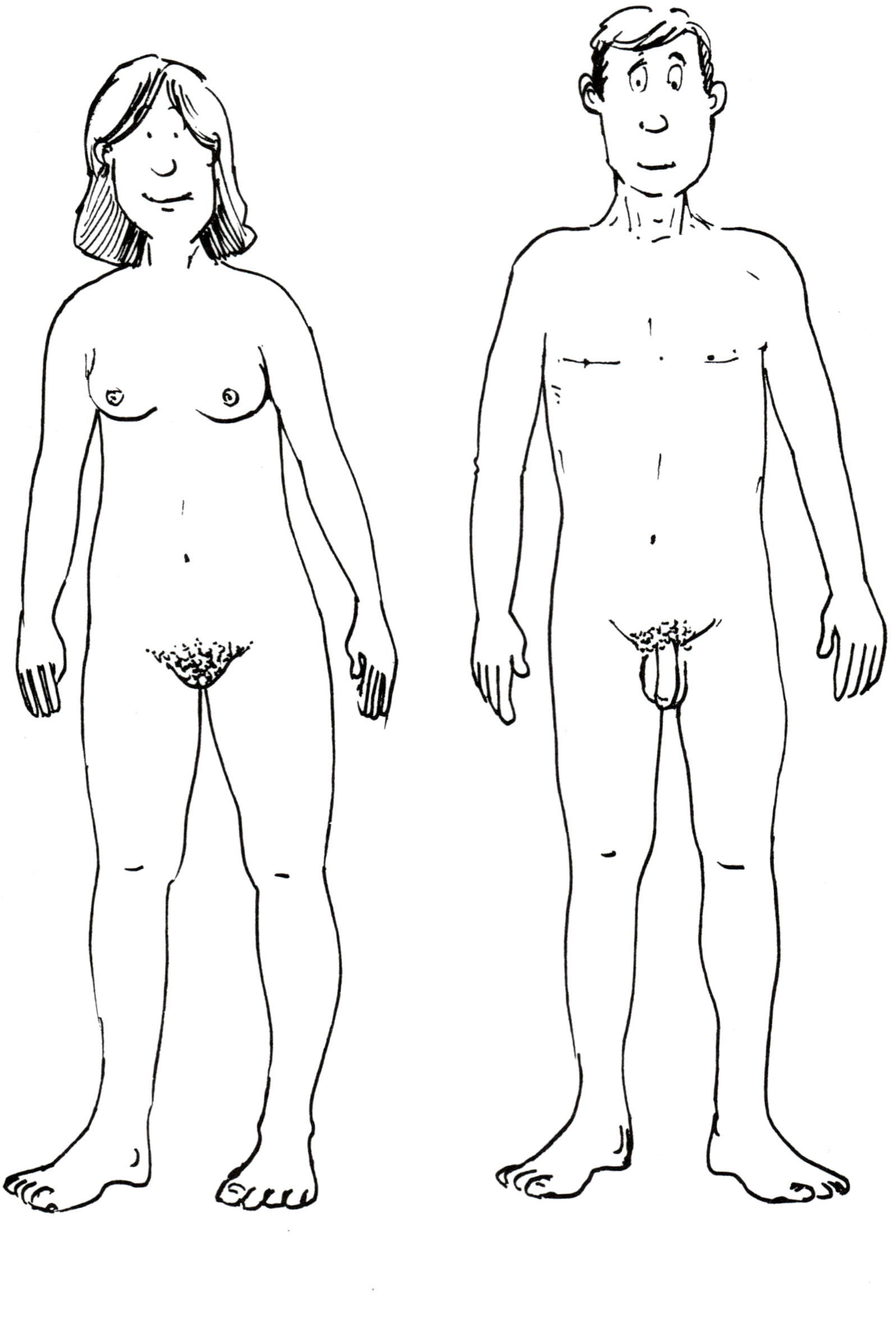

Personal routines

My name is ______________________. I am in class ______.

Things I need to do every day

- o
- o
- o
- o
- o

Things I need to do every week

- o
- o
- o
- o
- o

Things I need to do frequently

- o
- o
- o
- o
- o

C102

Environment wordsearch

a	b	c	d	e	f	g	h	i	j	k	l	m	n	o	p	q	r	s	t	u	v
e	c	o	l	o	g	i	c	a	l	w	x	y	z	a	b	c	d	e	f	g	h
c	b	a	z	y	x	w	v	u	n	t	s	r	q	p	o	n	m	i	k	j	l
u	e	f	g	h	i	j	k	i	l	m	n	e	x	h	a	u	s	t	o	r	p
l	i	h	g	f	e	d	a	c	b	a	z	y	x	w	v	u	t	s	e	r	q
t	l	m	n	o	p	r	q	r	s	t	u	v	w	x	y	z	a	y	b	c	d
r	w	v	u	t	d	s	r	q	p	o	n	m	l	k	j	l	a	h	g	f	e
a	z	a	b	i	c	d	e	f	g	h	r	l	j	k	i	l	m	m	n	o	p
v	h	g	c	f	e	d	c	b	a	z	a	y	x	w	e	v	u	t	s	r	q
i	c	a	r	b	o	n	d	i	o	x	i	d	e	n	k	l	m	n	o	p	e
o	h	g	f	e	d	c	b	a	z	y	n	x	o	w	v	u	t	s	r	e	q
l	k	l	m	n	o	p	q	r	s	t	f	z	u	v	w	x	y	z	r	q	b
e	u	t	s	r	q	p	o	n	m	l	o	k	j	i	h	g	f	f	e	d	c
t	x	y	g	l	o	b	a	l	w	a	r	m	i	n	g	z	d	a	b	c	d
x	w	v	u	t	s	r	q	p	o	n	e	m	l	k	j	a	i	h	g	t	e
y	z	n	a	b	c	d	e	f	g	h	s	i	j	k	e	l	m	n	o	p	q
f	e	d	u	c	b	a	z	y	p	e	t	r	o	l	x	w	v	u	t	s	r
g	h	i	j	c	k	l	m	n	o	c	p	q	r	s	t	u	v	w	x	y	z
m	l	k	p	o	l	l	u	t	i	o	n	j	i	h	g	f	e	d	c	b	a
n	o	p	q	r	s	e	t	u	r	s	w	x	y	z	a	b	c	d	e	f	g
v	q	p	o	n	m	l	a	k	j	y	i	h	c	h	e	m	i	c	a	l	s
s	t	u	v	w	x	y	z	r	a	s	b	c	d	e	f	g	h	i	j	k	l
g	f	e	d	c	b	a	z	y	x	t	w	v	u	t	s	r	q	p	o	n	m
o	i	l	s	p	i	l	l	h	i	e	x	t	i	n	c	t	i	o	n	j	k
f	e	d	c	b	a	z	y	x	w	m	v	u	t	s	r	q	p	o	n	m	i

Find the following words and then look up their meaning in the dictionary where necessary.

ecological
exhaust
acid rain
rainforest
carbon dioxide
ozone layer
lead free
pollution
nuclear
extinction
chemicals
petrol
global warming
ecosystem
oil spill
ultra violet

Titles

Title: ______________________

Imagine sitting in a car on a hot day. The windows are closed and the heat is building up with nowhere to escape.

POLLUTION

DESTROYING THE RAIN FORESTS

Title: ______________________

One day your Dad hangs out the washing and then goes off to burn garden rubbish. When your Mum returns she discovers soot all over the washing.

Title: ______________________

Last week all the children were very excited. They had heard that a new adventure playground was to be built were a cluster of trees, brambles and scrubland had once stood.

GREEN HOUSE EFFECT

WASTING ENERGY

Title: ______________________

Mum was furious. She came home to find the central heating on, the television flickering away, the cooker switched on, lights in the hallway and kitchen – and everyone playing the the garden.

Title: ______________________

When Bridie went to the beach on the first day of her holiday, her Mum told her to wear a T-shirt because of the fierce heat of the sun. Her T-shirt had a hole in it and she was badly sunburned.

ACID RAIN

Oxygen and smog

Making smog in the classroom

Measuring the amount of oxygen in the air

Classroom waste

Type of waste	Class numbers												Total weight for each type of waste
	Amount of waste (number of items)												
Total weight for all classrooms													

Protect your ears

Below are three types of ear protection. From the lists at the bottom of the page, choose a good point and a bad point for each of the types of protection shown. Write your choice in the box.

ear muffs 	Good points:
	Bad points:
ear plugs 	Good points:
	Bad points:
canal caps 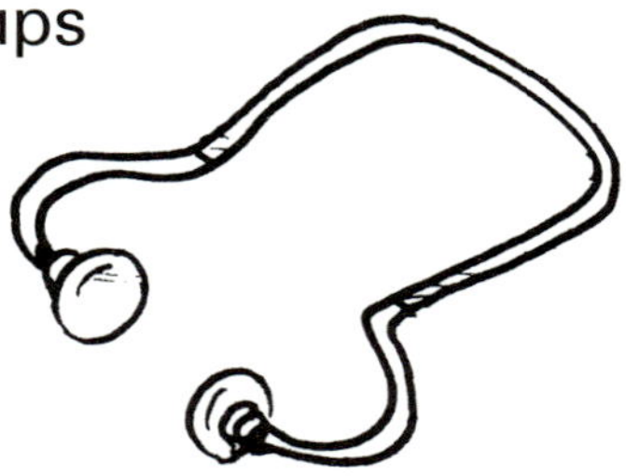	Good points:
	Bad points:

Good points

- are small, cheap, easy to carry and comfortable when the weather is hot
- are comfortable to wear and very light
- one size fits everyone and they provide the greatest protection

Bad points

- they don't always seal off the ear canal
- very bulky and can be hot to wear if the place is warm
- some can be hard to fit; if not cleaned than can introduce dirt into the ear canal.

Amrita and the trees

Ankle deep

What would happen if no rubbish from your home was ever gathered and collected?

Answer

What would happen if you didn't have a toilet or your toilet didn't work?

Answer

What would happen if there were no clean supply of water and you could not buy bottled water?

Answer

What would happen if the air you breathed in was polluted with smoke?

Answer

What would happen if people buried their rubbish (and even their dead) next to streams and rivers carrying the only supply of drinking water?

Answer

Western Europe

C109

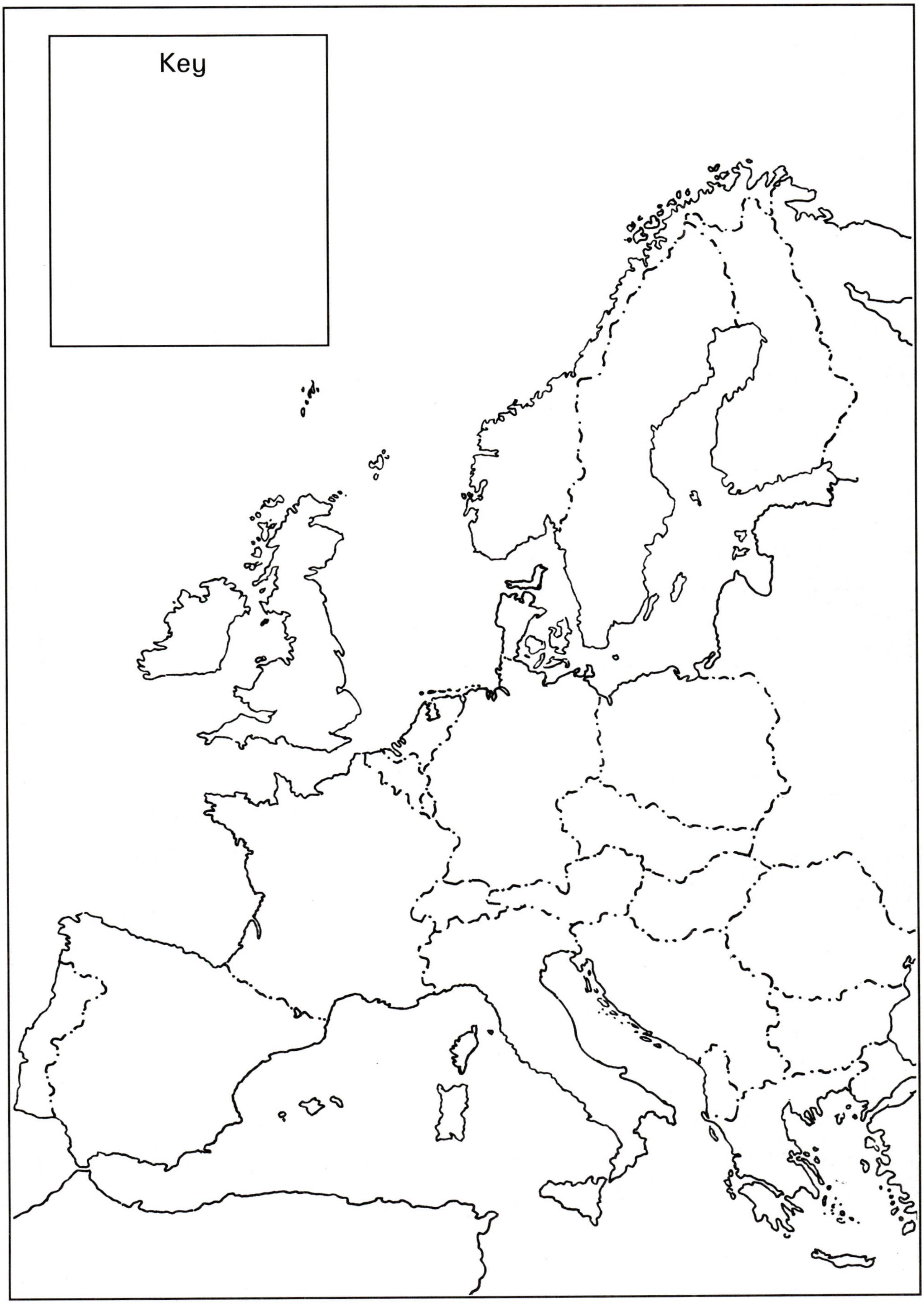

Environmental crimes

C110

Country	Water	Air	Waste	Chemical	Noise	Nature	**Total**
Spain	12	2	10	4	–	29	57
Belgium	11	3	18	5	2	7	46
Greece	10	4	6	2	3	20	45
France	15	3	2	1	–	20	41
Italy	9	4	10	2	3	12	40
United Kingdom	16	5	3	3	–	4	31
West Germany (now Germany)	9	4	2	3	–	11	29
Netherlands	6	2	2	3	3	8	24
Eire	7	2	3	2	–	7	21
Portugal	2	1	4	–	–	7	14
Luxembourg	5	2	2	–	1	2	12
Denmark	2	–	–	–	1	2	5
Total	104	32	62	25	13	129	362

Source: European Commission quoted in *The Green Wave – Sustainability*, 1990.

My best day

The things that make my best day are ...

My mind map

C112

The Peasants' Revolt

During the years 1337–1453, the English kings tried to regain lands they once held in France. Many battles took place during that time, although the English and French were not at war the whole time during that period that became known as The Hundred Years War.

Wars cost money and a poll tax, which claimed twelve day's wages, was imposed on each person. The poor people felt that they were being made to pay for the war, whereas the rich were avoiding paying at all. In addition to being free from this and other demands of their lords of the manor where they lived and worked, the poor people, referred to as peasants, also wanted to have more use of the forests.

Attacks against the landowners, certain churchmen and clerks who kept the records of the lord of the manor, began in Essex and Kent where most people lived. Much property was destroyed. The peasants united and marched to London for a confrontation with the landowners, government officials and lawyers who opposed them – but not the King who they believed was above this dispute.

First, led by a man called John Ball, they went to the Tower of London and although all was peaceful to begin with, the peasants murdered the Archbishop of Canterbury, the King's treasurer and the King's tax collector. From there they rioted through the streets of London, hurting people standing by and causing a great deal of damage. Finally, King Richard II agreed to meet them at his royal barge at Smithfield. There he agreed to their demands. However, one of the peasants' leaders, called Wat Tyler, argued with the Mayor of London who fought with him. The mayor killed Wat Tyler. The peasants were then persuaded to leave London. The promises made by Richard II were never kept. The Peasants failed to get the demands they had made.

Conflict (1)

Using copymaster 113 (The Peasants' Revolt), answer the following questions. Keep in mind how you might have solved the peasants' demands.

Name the two opposing sides, saying who was involved.

WHO IS INVOLVED?

WHAT DEMANDS ARE THERE?

List the demands of each side.

State which was the most important demand of each side.

Say which side caused the first incident and what happened.

THE INCIDENT

Name the most serious incidents in the story.

C115

Conflict (2)

Name any spokesmen or leaders.

THE LEADERS

Say who, if anyone, intervened (acted as a go-between) for the two sides.

THE GO-BETWEEN

Was there anything the two sides had in common?

COMMON GROUND

What happened that won or lost the claim made by either side?

If the two sides turned to you and said they would do whatever you decided depending on who you believed to be right, what would you do?

OPTIONS

ANSWER THIS QUESTION ON A SEPARATE PIECE OF PAPER

The community

Look carefully at the map. Find the following:

- library
- hospital
- school
- health centre
- factory/works
- recreation ground
- shopping parade
- church

When you find them colour them in and/or give their co-ordinates.

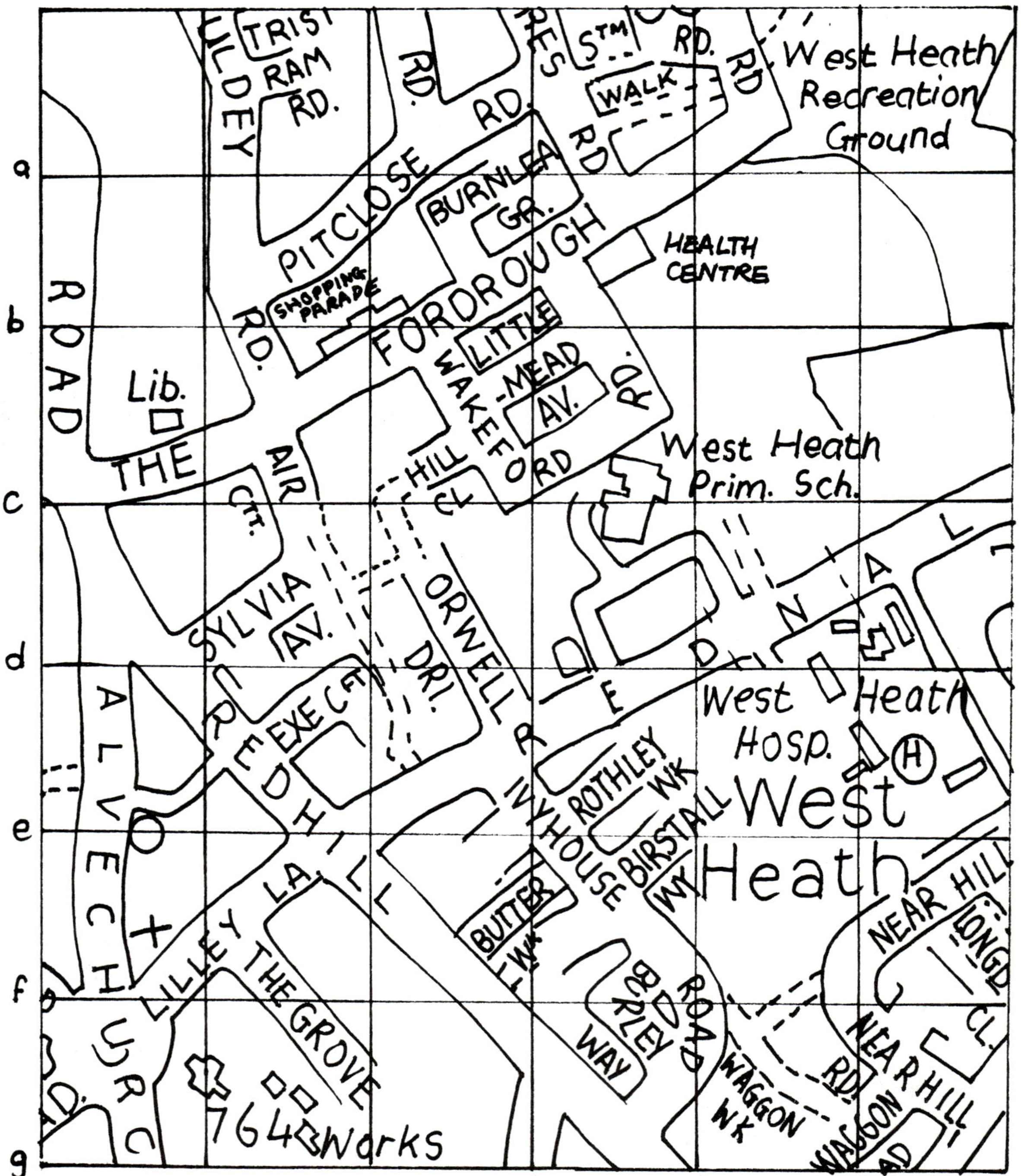

Source: A to Z Birmingham and West Midlands (Geographers Map Co. Ltd)

Community rules

Draw up rules aimed at encouraging people to care for your community. You may wish to create rules for neighbourhoods where people live: for play areas; for shopping areas; for factories and places of work; for schools.

COMMUNITY RULES

Name of Community ____________________

Signed ____________________

Date ____________________

Scary things

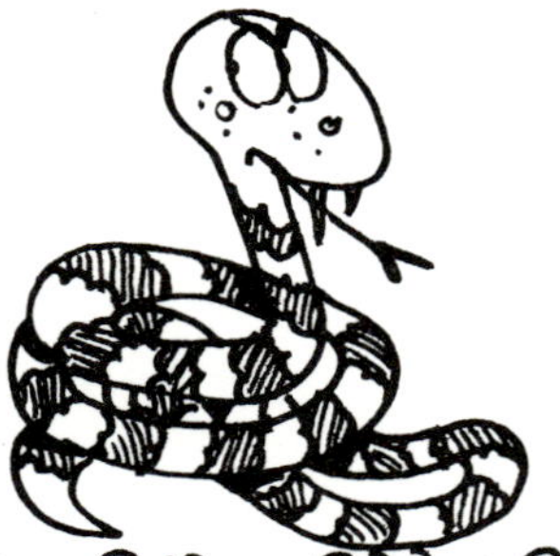

Things that go bump in the night!

Situation	What do I do … who do I tell?
 spider in the bathroom	
 a nightmare	
 a frightening TV programme	
 a bully	
 being approached by a stranger	
 crossing the road	
 being left at home all day	
 having to pass that chained-up dog	

Intro-extro

C120

Answer the questions below to find out if your personality is extrovert or introvert or some way towards either.

PERSONALITY TEST

	Yes	No
1) Do you like being in the company of friends?		
2) Do you like talking to adults?		
3) Do you easily become nervous?		
4) Do you tease others?		
5) Do you find loud laughter embarrassing?		
6) Do you hate practical jokes?		
7) Are you good at make excuses?		
8) Are you good at telling jokes?		
9) Would you rather stay in than go out?		
10) Do you like being on your own?		
11) Do you like going to parties?		
12) Do you like wearing bright clothes?		
13) Is it important for you to wear fashionable clothes		
14) Are you often in a bad mood?		
15) Are you afraid to answer questions in assembly?		

Transfer your answers on to the chart below and check them with those given by your teacher.

Yes															
Q	1	2	3	4	5	6	7	8	9	10	11	12	13	14	
No															

Trouble

Place a tick in the box next to the type of personality you think is most likely to be involved in the trouble shown.

Introvert		Extrovert	

Introvert		Extrovert	

Introvert		Extrovert	

Introvert		Extrovert	

Introvert		Extrovert	

Introvert		Extrovert	

Masks

happy side

sad side

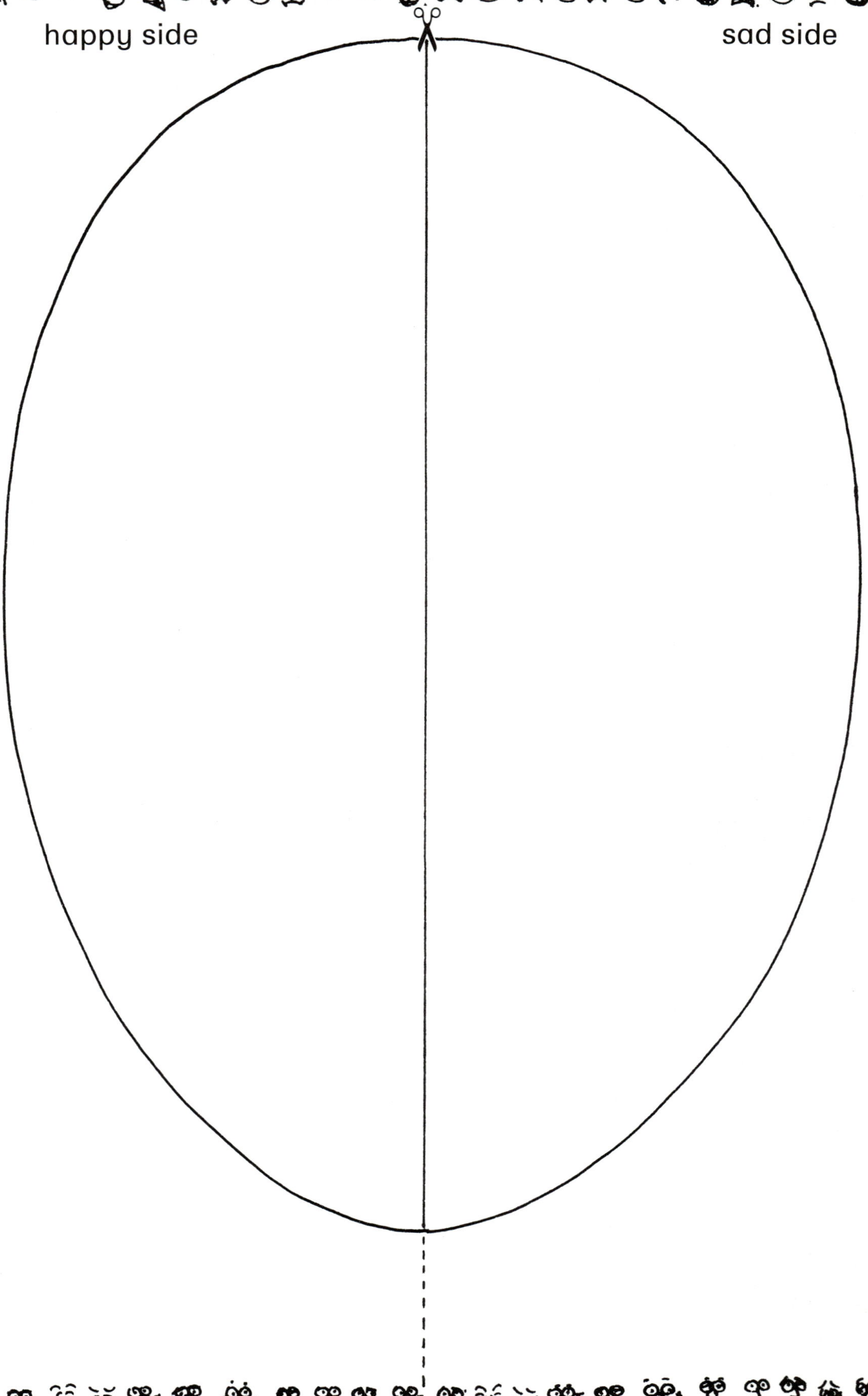

Things that worry me

C123

Complete the questionnaire either by yourself or asking others to do so. Place a 'Y' for yes or 'N' for no in the box next to the question. Find out which worries are the most common. Compare your results with others.

			Number of people 1	2	3	4	5
1)	I worry about my school work.	Q1					
2)	I worry about being bullied.	Q2					
3)	I worry about being told off by the teacher.	Q3					
4)	I worry about not looking good.	Q4					
5)	I worry about not being fashionable.	Q5					
6)	I worry about my shape.	Q6					
7)	I worry about my health.	Q7					
8)	I worry about standing out in assembly.	Q8					
9)	I worry about the neighbourhood where I live.	Q9					
10)	I worry that I don't have much money.	Q10					
11)	I worry about crossing the road.	Q11					
12)	I worry about people smoking.	Q12					
13)	I worry about going to secondary school.	Q13					
14)	I worry about not being liked.	Q14					
15)	I worry about how our house looks.	Q15					
16)	I worry about how our car looks.	Q16					
17)	I worry about what job I'll get.	Q17					
18)	I worry about how my Mum and Dad look.	Q18					
19)	I worry about how my hair looks.	Q19					
20)	I worry about how my skin looks.	Q20					

Temperament

FIERY PEOPLE
(lively, confident)

Name ______________________

I think this person is a fiery person because

____

____

____

____

____.

AIRY PEOPLE
(slow, day dreamers)

Name ______________________

I think this person is an airy person because

____

____

____

____

____

____

____.

Name ______________________

I think this person is an earthy person because

____

____

____

____

____

____

____

____

____.

EARTHY PEOPLE
(reliable, dependable, pratical)

Name ______________________

I think this person is a watery person because

____

____

____

____

____

____

____

____

____.

WATERY PEOPLE
(calm, slow, dull)